PRINT
MAGIC

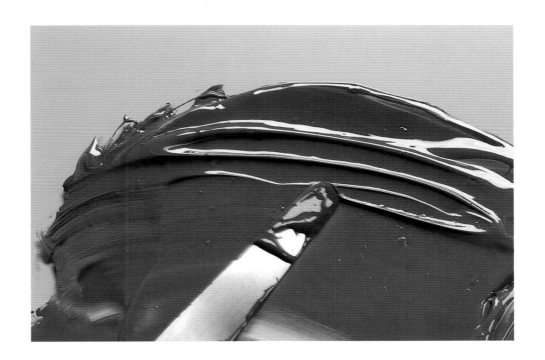

PRINT
MAGIC

THE COMPLETE GUIDE TO
DECORATIVE PRINTING TECHNIQUES

JOCASTA INNES &
STEWART WALTON

PHOTOGRAPHY BY GRAHAM RAE

AURUM PRESS

First published 1997 by Aurum Press Ltd.,
25 Bedford Avenue, London WC1B 3AT

Original Photography: Graham Rae
Art Direction and Design: David Fordham
Project Editor: Judy Spours
Styling: Leeann MacKenzie
Picture Research: Emily Hedges

A catalogue record for this book is available from the
British Library.

ISBN 1 85410 475 6

Manufactured in China by Imago

ACKNOWLEDGEMENTS

The authors and publishers would like to thank the
following for their help with the preparation of this book:

Josh George

Ros Greenbaum

Madhu McChrystal

Katherine Morris, 2 Matthew's Yard, Shorts Gardens,
London WC2H 9HR

The Staff of the St Bride's Printing Library, Bride Lane,
London EC4

CONTENTS

INTRODUCTION

P RINTING, ESSENTIALLY, is about making a mark, informative or decorative, frequently both, which can be easily replicated. The means, tools and intentions of a printing process are as various as the surfaces to be printed – paper, cloth, ceramics, glass, plastic. Nowadays printing technology is a highly sophisticated form of mass-production, offering countless ways of transferring words, patterns, photographs or art, both in the form of reproductions or as 'artists' prints', onto a given surface. Desk-top publishing allows anyone with computer skills to be their own printer. Printing of one sort or another is so deeply woven into contemporary life that any interruption to it – a newspaper strike, a blip in the photocopier – causes alarm and frustration. In this multi-media context it needs an effort of the imagination to trace the process back to its primary impulse, but if nothing else this journey illuminates the distance we have travelled and underlines the special role of the printed, as distinct from the drawn or painted, mark.

If the first art was palaeolithic, a sure and economical depiction of animals on cave walls, to celebrate a successful hunt, to propitiate animal spirits, or simply for identification purposes, the first prints, often seen accompanying the paintings, were handprints, sprinkled around like a frieze. These may be the artists' or the tribal witnesses' and we cannot tell what their significance was, but we can legitimately infer that in making them, dipping their hands in puddled clay or blood or soot and pressing them onto the cave walls, the actors in this particular scenario had already discovered two distinguishing features of the printing process: ease of application and speed of replication. Also, perhaps, they experienced the joyous satisfaction in using the simplest means and materials to make significant marks. All of these seem to me to underlie the evolution of printing throughout its complex ramifications over history, and to a large extent those considerations have influenced the choice of printing processes described and illustrated in this book.

OPPOSITE *A dazzling array of raw pigment dyes in Hanoi, Vietnam (above) and in Karnataka, India (below).* RIGHT *An improvised print room in the home of the celebrated Swedish artist and illustrator Carl Larsson, in 1910.*

7

This is not intended as a reference book for specialists but rather as a primer for people of a creative bent who may not be aware of the visual enrichment that printing, even at the simplest level, can offer, when presented with a little guidance about suitable designs and materials and with considerable encouragement in the shape of what they can achieve. When so many printing processes, like photocopying, have made rapid reproduction tediously mechanical, there is a rare and special satisfaction to be found in going back to square one, carving a potato into a simple but effective stamp, inking it and printing it onto paper or fabric. This is a bit more advanced than handprints, but not so much so as to be daunting. It teaches you a lot about making satisfying patterns from simple elements, about the surprise that different colour combinations can deliver, and about the soothing pleasure of watching an idea grow over a roll of paper or cloth, controlled, deliberate, your own creation.

We have interpreted the idea of printing loosely in this book, guided by a sense of what is achievable by untrained people without too much outlay for specialist tools and equipment. A purist might object to the inclusion of resist dyeing – batik, for instance – which is largely based on freehand drawing on cloth with melted wax, though block-printing with melted wax, or *tjap*, grew up alongside hand-drawn batik. Tie dye, likewise, is a sort of negative printing, more random and less controlled than printing in its strict sense. But both are delightfully effective and popular ways to turn a length of plain, cheap cloth into a lovely thing, and that seemed to us close to the spirit if not the letter of printing.

Stencilling is not strictly a printing process either, though as a simple means of replication of a design, stencils are closer to the root impulse behind printing. However, it seemed appropriate to include them because they were so intimately involved at various stages of printing history, as in early printed decorative papers – *papiers domino* – and woodcut book illustrations, as a fast if sometimes hasty and crude way to add colour to black-and-white images and patterns. Also, without some grounding in the cutting and colour differentiation involved in building up a complex coloured stencil, readers might find the screen printing process rather hard to grasp.

Similarly, we have been catholic in our choice of materials and media. Most shown here, widely used by professionals for their convenience, are readily available, fast-drying, inexpensive – and they reflect a growing move towards water-based, acrylic media rather than the more traditional oil-based media (screen printing is a clear example). However, in certain instances, as with indigo dyeing, we felt it was allowable to introduce a note of traditional mystique. You can buy a satisfactory synthetic indigo dyestuff, but where a process has achieved such splendid results over centuries it seemed a pity to leave it out, even though it takes understanding and patience to use it successfully. The point of all how-to books is to fire your imagination and get you going, and sometimes it is the byways of a process rather than the technique as such which does so.

THE HISTORY OF PRINTING

THE HISTORY OF PRINTING begins with the simple discovery that a relief surface, like the human palm, can transfer itself with seductive ease and speed to any reasonably flat surface. From this little acorn, over many millennia, a gigantic oak has grown in fits and starts, fed by advances and discoveries in other fields of human activity, sometimes nearly related, sometimes quite remote, but always with efficacy as a priority. Printing techniques have attracted major artists, as well as brilliant designers, since their first appearance, and it would be simplistic to suggest that their only interest in the processes was crudely commercial and driven by the wish to multiply their images speedily and efficiently, to appeal to a wider market. The technical challenge, and discipline, of mastering a new printing

This view of three trees silhouetted against a stormy sky is an excellent example of the sumptuous blacks obtained by the etching process in the hands of a master like Rembrandt (1606-69).

process – etching, engraving, lithography, screen printing – provided an exciting stimulus which developed another facet of their creative personality. We would be impoverished, aesthetically, if Rembrandt, Dürer, Goya, Daumier, Picasso, and many many others, had not tried their hand at exploring the possibilities of printing, in one form or another, as a conduit for ideas and images which demanded a vivid, graphic, different expression from the large-scale, more slowly developed, process of painting.

However, having acknowledged the special role printing processes have played in the fine arts, it still seems broadly true that printing, in all its ramifications, has been primarily a trade, a commercial enterprise driven like any other by the need to increase efficiency, speed production, cut overheads and notch up larger profits. This has made it, on the whole, responsive to technological advances and scientific discoveries. A family's fortunes might be founded by a shrewd entrepreneur, like Benjamin Franklin with his ink manufacturing in the USA, or the Rothschilds with

their printed textiles dispatched all over Europe during the nineteenth century; even, to a minor extent, the founders of batik printing workshops in Java, or village workshops for *bhandana* printing in rural India. Because printing processes are essentially to do with large and rapid turnover, there was money to be made in one area or another, which makes it the more paradoxical that the father of letterpress, the German goldsmith-cum-inventor Johann Gutenberg, died in relative obscurity and poverty, thus confirming the business adage that innovators take the risk and their imitators collect the profits.

Printing nowadays subsumes so many specialized skills and processes, from cottage industry to mega industrial plants, and the terminology used is so confusing to a layperson, that it seems sensible and helpful to begin with a brief definition of the historically important printing categories and innovations, especially those relevant to this book.

RELIEF PRINTING

THE FIRST PRINTING TECHNIQUE to be developed was relief printing, from carved wooden blocks. Originally used to decorate textiles, these were used to print block books with text and illustrations in China around the eighth century AD. Almost certainly, examples would have reached Europe along the trade routes and caused a ripple of wonderment, probably as much to do with their incomprehensible script of characters as with the technical novelty they embodied. It must have been clear to any contemporary with a speculative turn of mind that here was an idea worth considering. On the other hand, to carve a page of text, never mind hundreds, in mirror-writing, so that it would print positively, would have been a slow and costly undertaking, even if the blocks could print off thousands of impressions. Besides, they may have argued, where was the market for block books? The literate classes, nobles, monks and so forth, could afford to pay scribes to copy religious texts, romances, poems or songs, and the rest of society relied on oral

A French compositor in 1850, dressed in his work smock, is in the process of making up a line of type from boxes of cast-metal founts.

tradition for information and entertainment. However, the seed of an incalculably powerful idea had been sown in the European mind, and this germinated slowly, finding nourishment in a wide range of parallel discoveries and innovations, in textile and decorative paper printing, in engraving on armour and precious metals, in the development of paints and varnishes which, unlike the Chinese block book inks, would not wash off, stain or fade.

Relief printing from wood blocks was well established and understood by the time, in mid-fifteenth-century Germany, that Johann Gutenberg made his conceptual leap forward. His invention, moveable type, was made up of individual lead letters cast in relief, and in the mirror-writing negative mode, so that lines of text could be made up, or composed – the man who did this was a 'compositor' – in a wooden frame, or 'forme'. When a page of text had been completed, it was inked up, and printed off under pressure onto paper. Because the type was made up of individually cast letters (the use of punches and dies in his goldsmithing is thought to have suggested this) any words or texts could be endlessly re-printed once the compositor had done his work.

The individual letters were made by leaving each one in relief and then striking, or sinking, it into a slab of brass to make a matrix, or mould, into which molten lead was poured to make the type letters. Thousands of individual letters would have been needed for an entire book. One of the difficulties first encountered, which Gutenberg solved, was how to cast the letters so that the composed lines of type, standing on the level bed of the press, presented a uniformly flat surface for printing. The screw-and-lever press used by Gutenberg is thought to have been modelled on a wine press.

Within fifteen years of Gutenberg's death in 1468, printing presses had been set up throughout most of Europe. Astonishingly, the first type founts were modelled on the handwritten scripts of the day, making the first printed incunabula (from the Latin for cradle, meaning early or infant books) virtually indistinguishable from their handwritten predecessors. It was another fifty years before the first plethora of typefaces crystallized into one of two directions, towards the so-called Roman and Italic, based on allegedly classical forms, or towards the Gothic or black-letter type then used for script in Germany and parts of northern Europe. Though these established norms for typeface for centuries to come, every generation or so has produced a type designer who has modified the prevailing founts to create a subtly, sometimes minutely, different type, sometimes an affair of altering the spacing of letters rather than changing the shape of the letters themselves. But though typeface altered fractionally, and automated processes speeded up printing processes enormously, most books until as recently as the 1950s were still produced by 'letterpress', the generic term for negative relief printing. Nowadays far more rapid processes, such as offset litho and photo-typesetting, are standard, though traditional letterpress is still used for quality printing, not only of special books but for such items as stationery, invitations and cards, where the richer texture and blackness of the print adds an unmistakable touch of class.

A box of cast metal type, mainly capitals and numerals, from a contemporary hand-printing press.

While relief printing by letterpress was undoubtedly the most revolutionary, and widely influential, innovation in printing history, ultimately launching information technology as we know it today, it was only one form of relief printing, and there have been others, stemming from decorative block printing and carved woodblocks. Lino cuts are a twentieth-century version, but the primitive potato cut is another cheap and ancient printing tool, capable of ingenious manipulation for quite sophisticated results (*see* p. 37). Both of these accessible, and unfrightening, relief printing tools are excellently suited to beginners who want to try their skills at designing and printing without elaborate or expensive setting-up costs.

INTAGLIO

No RESUMÉ, however brief, of printing methods and processes would be complete without a mention of 'intaglio' printing techniques, and a description of how these differ from relief printing. Intaglio is an Italian word meaning to carve out a design from a flat surface, in the manner of the old seals and signet rings in which

a scooped out motif, impressed on hot soft wax, left a raised image. Jelly moulds are a simple analogue. The first intaglio process to become widely used was engraving, usually on copper, where the artist incised his drawing with a sharp pointed tool, or burin, into the metal. After clearing away any roughness or burrs, the plate was inked, then cleaned off to leave the ink only in the incised lines. The plate was then laid on the press, and a sheet of paper, dampened to make it stretchy and malleable, laid on top. When the press was lowered and tightened, the softened paper was forced into the inked incisions of the engraved design to leave a clean, sharp, and subtly heightened – literally, though microscopically – image.

Engraving allows much finer execution than woodcuts, and its introduction in the eighteenth century led to a new sophistication in print making right across the board. Etching is an offshoot of engraving, where the design is incised into a wax layer on top of a copper plate, and the plate then treated with acid, which eats into the non-waxed areas. It is then printed in much the same way. Wood engraving, another intaglio process, is a sort of woodcut in negative. Thomas Bewick (1755–1828), the North-umberland-born artist engraver famous for his finely detailed vignettes of birds, animals and country scenes, is credited with perfecting the wood engraving technique. Whereas woodcuts, or blocks, are carved from the 'plank' side of a piece of wood, wood engraving is done on the end grain of fine-textured woods like box, holly, lime, which are hard enough to allow the most delicate incised detail to register.

None of these 'intaglio' printing techniques is as straightforward as relief printing methods, which is why they have been excluded from this book. Quite apart from the skills and experience needed to execute them competently, there is the added difficulty of working almost invisibly, though artists in these media have tricks for showing up their work, like coating a wood engraving block with white paint. And mistakes cannot be corrected – one slip of the engraver's burin and the plate is indelibly scarred. Their appeal to artists with an interest in printing is in the finely detailed, but juicily printed, images they deliver. The difference between an artist's numbered proof in any of these media and a photo-litho reproduction is small, to a casual eye, but significant on a closer inspection – a difference of intensity, sharpness and vitality.

MONOTYPE

WHILE RELIEF AND INTAGLIO printing are recognizably printing processes to a lay mind, there are other allied ones which fulfil the basic definition of printing as a means of replication, while making use of completely different tools, methods and materials. Monotype is interesting today chiefly because it was the process adopted by William Blake (1757–1827) for his radiantly beautiful series called 'The Large Colour

Prints' of twelve Biblical subjects. In monotype the subject was painted directly onto a plate or block in oil colour, which then was printed off under pressure. Mono means, of course, one, and monotype prints were close to being one-offs, though as many as three prints of some Blake subjects are recorded. The prints gained a mysterious depth and richness of colour through the mingling of paints in the printing process, and were intended to be finished by hand. Blake, a rare example of poet and artist working as one towards a visionary purpose, was excited by medieval manuscripts with their counterpoint of handwritten script and painted illumination, and his two lovely books of poems and coloured illustrations, *Songs of Innocence* and *Songs of Experience*, were consciously designed to give something of the same immediacy and intimacy, the lettering and drawings printed as etchings, with colour added by hand, mostly, it is said, by his tolerant and devoted wife.

Etched and hand-coloured plate of the poem 'The Little Boy Found' from Songs of Innocence *by William Blake, dating from c. 1815–26.*

Lithograph of a Butcher's Shop by Eric Ravilious, one of his delightful illustrations to the book High Street *by J. M. Richards, published in 1938.*

LITHOGRAPHY

LITHOGRAPHY, which became widely popular in the latter half of the nineteenth century, chiefly as a sophisticated means of colour reproduction, is what is called a planographic process, that is, the printing relies neither on relief or intaglio but is all on the same 'plane'. In lithography, a slab of smooth limestone acts as the plate, so to speak, the design being drawn directly onto the stone with a greasy crayon. The completed design is treated with acid and gum arabic to fix the image, then the stone is wetted. When an inked roller is drawn across the stone the colour adheres only to the greasy image and is repelled by the wet stone. The successive impressions, one for each colour, are taken off in a rolling process. Most artists who have essayed print-making have worked 'on the stone', from Degas, Cézanne, Renoir and Matisse to more recent names like Paul Nash and Eduardo Paolozzi.

For the purposes of this book, however, the chief interest of lithography is a certain family resemblance to that specifically twentieth-century process, screen printing. To some extent screen printing is planographic too, since only enough manual pressure is needed to force the printing ink through a fine mesh screen, through stencils, onto the surface to be printed. What it lacks in dynamism, the juicy richness of an imprint, it makes up for in ease, speed and compactness. Once the principle of stencil overlays is grasped (*see* p. 125), registering each colour precisely, this ingenious, but essentially simple, tool allows considerable scope for experiment and gives fast, slick and professional-looking repeats on a wide variety of surfaces. These qualities have made printing screens popular among most contemporary artists and print-makers, and standard equipment in art schools; indeed, thanks to their simplicity, in school art classes, too.

INKS

NOWADAYS, with such a wide choice of media available to anyone embarking on a printing project, selecting a suitable ink, dye or paint may seem to be merely a secondary concern, almost an afterthought. Historically, however, the medium was as important as the process itself. Gutenberg's cast metal type, for instance, would have been useless without the oleo-resinous ink he researched and perfected to print with. The water-based inks used by earlier block book printers simply reticulate on metal. Gutenberg was fortunate in being able to draw on work done by contemporary artists, notably Van Eyck, on oil-based paints and varnishes. The ink Gutenberg developed for printing his incunabula is still generally regarded as faultless, and has never been bettered. He did not publish the recipe, doubtless recognizing its commercial value, but ink recipes surviving from a later date suggest that it must have included some of the following ingredients: linseed oil, turpentine, Venice turpentine (a natural resin) and both hard and liquid varnishes. Liquid varnish was made from oil and gum sandarac. Black pigment was largely supplied by pitch or lampblack, with the possible addition of iron pyrites (ferric sulphide).

Printers, like painters and colour-men, had to be their own chemists, and there is plenty of evidence that the recipe for a successful ink was a fiercely guarded trade secret. Its manufacture often took place in public, outside the city walls, because the lengthy cooking up of the various ingredients must have given off powerful, and probably toxic, fumes. As with alchemy, ink-making was mysterious; rumours circulated that crusts of stale bread and raw onions tossed into the ink kettle at the right moment resulted in a superior ink which would print clean, crisp and black, without staining or fading gradually to brown. A poor ink left black smudges, known as 'monks', on the paper, and white spots, 'friars', on the letters.

Ink was made in a two-handed kettle, usually of copper, with a close-fitting lid. Round bottomed, it needed a thick wreath of straw to stand on when taken from the fire. An iron bar or spatula was used to stir the mixture as new ingredients were added. A sharp stick or fork held the crusts and raw onions. Opinion remains divided as to whether these outlandish additions really improved the brew. However, the wooden sticks certainly acted like a crude thermometer: when charred they indicated that the ink had reached the right temperature. German printmakers evolved their own macho ritual, frying bread rolls in the hot linseed oil, washed down with a shot of Schnapps to cut the grease. It is no surprise to learn that this printer's perk was an acquired taste. Nor is it surprising to discover that wind was the great hazard to the process, and that there was an ever present risk of fire. According to Hansard, one of the most serious London fires, in 1820, was caused by ink-making. Most of the ingredients are highly flammable, the kettle was unstable, the handles were burning hot; one false move, a splash on the fire, and the stage was set for a terrifying flare-up.

A good black ink on display in a wonderfully vigorous woodcut of 1909 by Raoul Dufy, illustrating a poem by Apollinaire.

A GOOD BLACK INK

As the demand for printed matter intensified, so did the commercial value of a good, black ink. Successful ink-makers became rich. Benjamin Franklin was the first American ink manufacturer, before he entered politics. The need to protect a proven recipe reached such a pitch that in one famous English firm, Whittinghams, the formulation for their super black ink was known only to the firm's boss, who let only one person, his nephew, into the secret and insisted on preparing it in a small back room in the printworks to which he and his nephew held the only keys. By this time, in the early nineteenth century, the quasi-alchemical aura surrounding early ink manufacture had given place to hard-nosed, commercial realism.

However, the search for a good black ink continued, driven by shrewd entrepreneurs. The first published work on the subject, by William Savage, printer to the Royal Institution, entitled *On Printing Ink, both Black and Coloured*, did not appear till 1832.

Previously, the quest for a good, permanent, glossy black led to considerable experiment, with various sources of black pigment being explored and tested.

LE CHAT.

Je souhaite dans ma maison :
Une femme ayant sa raison,
Un chat passant parmi les livres,
Des amis en toute saison
Sans lesquels je ne peux pas vivre.

None of these were readily available over the counter, so the ink-making process began at square one, with attempts to discover the ideal 'black'. Lampblack, the cheapest and most commonly used source, was made by igniting pitch resin in an iron vessel over which a frame covered with sheepskin was stretched to catch the fall-out. Peach black, ivory black and Frankfurt black were made in a similar fashion, by heating the various ingredients – peach stones, ivory or bone, vine prunings – in a crucible till they were reduced to black ashes. The raw material, or pigment, could be ruined by inadequate 'mulling', the manual process by which coarse or impure pigment is ground to ideal fineness by working it with a 'muller' of glass, marble or porphyry on a smooth slab. At a time when all artists made up their own paints (or employed an apprentice to do so) to their own 'secret' specifications, such laborious groundwork would not have seemed out of the way. A 'good black', neither staining nor spotting, could make a firm's fortune.

Various refinements were introduced. It was recognized that linseed oil, made from grinding flax seeds, needed to stand or mature for at least a year for impurities to settle out. Linseed oil was always a double-edged sword for fine artists, because though desirably tough and durable as well as oleaginous, it darkened and yellowed over time, but for printers seeking a 'good black' this would have been irrelevant. Prussian blue pigment was sometimes added to the standard black for 'bloom', and as a strong drier. Curiously enough, William Morris (1834–96), during his Kelmscott Press phase, dedicated to reinstating the beauty and integrity of medieval illuminated and hand-scripted texts, became convinced of the efficacy of stale bread and raw onion as an ingredient of a super ink/varnish, together with the addition of natural turpentine after at least six months' 'ripening'. An example of the wheel turning full circle, perhaps? Nowadays, printing inks come in many forms and different media, keeping pace with a host of technological changes, but the ideal 'good black' remains elusive, unimportant for most commercial purposes but a sort of alchemist's stone in the realm of fine letterpress.

PAPER

THE INVENTION OF PAPER followed on from an earlier, and crucial, invention of a camel's hair brush. We owe both inventions to Chinese scholars. The brush was the brain-child of Meng L'ien, in 250 BC. Previously the writing tool was a sharpened stick. The brush, used with an ink made from lampblack bound with gum, made it possible to write on delicate materials, such as silk, and Chinese hand-painted scrolls were the ancestors of books as we know them. The discovery that macerated vegetable fibre, compressed into leaves or sheets, equalled paper was made some three centuries later, in AD 105, by Ts'ai Lin, a court eunuch. Presumably this new and useful material continued in use for brush paintings and scrolls; but another five hundred years elapsed before paper met print, in the form of the first block books.

Meanwhile, other cultures had come up with their own, local solutions to the problem of finding a light (remember, early treaties and proclamations were either carved in stone, or cast in bronze, permanent but hardly portable), flexible, smooth-surfaced material on which scribes could copy texts, or a ruler's edicts for promulgation up and down the land. None of these alternatives answered the brief as satisfactorily as Ts'ai Lin's pressed sheets of macerated vegetable fibre, but many were ingenious, and the sheer variety of solutions testifies to an imperious, universal requirement. Information technology was already on the move.

ALTERNATIVE MATERIALS

PAPYRUS WAS THE SOLUTION developed in Ancient Egypt, using a local material, the tall jointed reeds that figure in many Egyptian wall paintings. Papyrus 'paper' was made by joining thin slices of reeds, patchwork fashion, to make up a thin 'board'. The idea seems cumbersome compared with the Chinese rag paper. Probably we all remember papyrus because it is the etymological root word from which our own 'paper' derives.

Vellum, or parchment, was the writing surface most widely favoured in Europe from early times, and it must be one of those freakish accidents of history that we have ended up with an inaccurate Early Egyptian term to describe paper, a Chinese invention, though 'vellum' lingers on in a small way as a trade description of a superior quality paper. Vellum was made from the inner layers of animal hides, usually sheep or calf. The skins were split, after treatment in lime pits to remove hair and impurities. The grain or wool side became 'skiver', or leather (used in turn for binding books), and the flesh side parchment or vellum. Slaked lime not only cleaned the hides (the lime putty was then used to make 'haired' plaster and render for building purposes) but gave them a dry, papery feel, removing any oil, grease or moisture, a consequence which anyone who has handled lime products can vouch for as they re-grease their parched and papery hands. Before being put up for sale, the fine, creamy, somewhat translucent hides were given a final scraping down and smoothing with pumice stone. Vellum provided a delicious writing surface for quill pen or brush, a suspicion that the loving elaboration of detail and script in early manuscripts such as the Book of Kells seems to confirm. When 'books' were handwritten, luxury items restricted to the rich and powerful, vellum was more than adequate. However, once printing, in our sense of the word, was launched on the world, vellum would have proved impossibly expensive.

Before going on to look at the development of paper-making in Europe, it seems worth recording some of the other materials that were used in different parts of the world. Roman schoolboys wrote, or rather scratched, with a stylus, on thin wooden boards covered with wax, chalk or plaster. The Roman historian Diodorus Siculus mentions that the judges of Syracuse scratched the names of persons sentenced to banishment on the silvery underside of olive leaves, somewhat in the style of today's office memos. The Singalese used palm leaves, which dry to a soft greenery-yallery shade, to make elegant little books in a 'landscape' format. In Assam, aloe leaves were used, the incised inscriptions being filled in with black pigment. Interestingly, this use of black pigment to fill incised designs had a counterpart in the European metalworker's technique, *niello,* where engraved designs and inscriptions were thrown into prominence by infilling with black wax or pitch-based varnish, now thought to have been a direct ancestor of 'intaglio' printing methods, and a possible influence on Gutenberg himself.

One last local writing surface is worth mentioning – the use of bark, which some trees shed in fine papery curls. The American Indians used birch bark to write on. The interest, and relevance, of bark as paper comes from the Latin name for bark, *liber,* which is clearly the root of our own 'library'.

PAPER-MAKING

PAPER-MAKING is one of those specialized trades which has evolved its own vocabulary. Thus the key figures involved in paper-making in Britain from the sixteenth century were known as vatmen, couchers and laymen. The macerating fibres, or 'stock', are heated in a 'pistolet', or large vat, kept constantly stirred or agitated to prevent the heavier, fibrous material settling to the bottom. The vatman scoops up 'stock' onto a mould, and shakes it to distribute the sludgy stuff evenly, then passes it to the coucher, whose job is to drain it and reverse the contents at the right moment onto a piece of felting. Then the layman becomes responsible for applying mechanical pressure to squeeze out any surplus moisture before the gradual drying out and sorting of the pressed sheets into piles, quires (24 sheets) and posts (144 sheets – 6 quires). A ream, from the Arab word *rizmah* meaning bundle, numbers 480 sheets (20 quires). Deckle-edged refers to the frame or 'deckle' into which the wet fibre sheet is first pressed, any surplus running up its sides to give the characteristic uneven, wavy edges, a clear indica-tion of paper being handmade and top quality.

Compared with printers, paper-makers come into a semi-skilled category, performing routine tasks which require judgement and experience, certainly, but not independent decision-making. Physically, however, it was a more demanding process than one might imagine, and this description by a teenage apprentice, Ebenezer Hiram Steadman, of his duties in his father's paper mill in Lexington, Massachusetts, gives an insight into a world of work unimaginable today.

From January until May I would have to get up in the mornings at 2 o'clock, the first thing was to make a fire to warm the water in the vat where they dipt up the pulp to form sheets of paper. I had to go into a hole on my hands and knees, ten feet long by three feet square, to make a fire in what was called a pot. The smoke came out of the hole and this was on the outside of the mill. Exposed to the weather in winter no one will ever realize how much I suffered with cold, snow, rain and smoke. Many times I have had to hold my breath while making the fire and dodge in for a chance to put in a stick of wood, then back out for the space was too small to turn around. After making the fire then I would have to wake up the vatman and the coucher and the other workmen in the paper mill.

PICTURES OF THE FLOATING WORLD

O NE OF THE MOST BRILLIANT episodes in the history of relief printing on paper is the intense flowering between the mid-eighteenth and nineteenth centuries of Japanese woodblock prints. When they first began arriving in Europe, reportedly used as wrapping paper for export porcelain, they were a revelation, eagerly collected by artists, and their

'The Great Wave of Kanagawa' by Katsushika Hokusai, published as one of the series '36 Views of Mount Fuji' in 1831. It is one of the most famous of all the Japanese floating world colour woodblock prints.

influence on art and design was pervasive and lasting. Quite apart from their aesthetic merits, there was something astonishing and unprecedented in so much technical skill and fastidious craftsmanship being lavished on a form of popular art, printed on fragile sheets of paper. Everything about these prints was surprising: their exotic subject-matter, fresh and vivid colour, arresting composition, exquisite detail. At a time when academic European art seemed to be running out of steam, stifled under aspic-like glazes, here suddenly was a fascinatingly different, mysteriously beautiful, boldly sophisticated product from the other side of the world, and people were enthralled.

Given the language difficulties, exacerbated by Japan's centuries-long isolation from world events, it must have been some time before anything much was known about the artists whose personal seals, often accompanied by a short poem, or *haiku*, identified these works. But gradually some names – Hiroshige, Utamaro, Hokusai, Harunobu – worked their way into Western consciousness, although they were but a handful of the scores of gifted artists who worked in the genre. Even today research continues to throw up work of quality by previously unidentified artists. But if the detail remains incomplete, the broad picture is clear.

UKIYO-E

JAPANESE WOODBLOCK PRINTS go under the generic title of *ukiyo-e,* which translates as 'pictures of a floating world'. This has nothing to do with the fact that boats and water figure in so many of the prints. It is believed to derive, distantly, from the Buddhist concept of life as illusion, transient, and goes back to a time when most Japanese art was an expression of religious beliefs. The *ukiyo-e* prints did not spring from a cultural vacuum. A long tradition of painting, both secular and religious, on screens and scrolls, as well as a remarkable tradition of Zen ink paintings, much influenced by Chinese examples, lay behind its development. So too did a level of specialist craftsmanship in carving, printing and paper-making which has rarely been matched.

However, there was nothing mystical about the 'floating world pictures', which record, with unabashed hedonism, the daily and ordinary life of 'old Japan', delivering something of a culture shock to the average Westerner. The earliest as well as most consistently popular work in the tradition was erotic; mildly erotic as in the series of *bijin-ga,* or 'beautiful girl prints' ('pin-ups' we would call them) or explicitly so in the *shunga,* or virtual sex manuals, showing lovers coupling in all the forty-eight positions recognized by Japanese amatory tradition. No shame attached to either the design, production or sale of erotica, and most of the famous artists of their day produced series of wood-blocks in the genre, as elegant as they are explicit.

However, though erotica may have been the most commercially successful subject undertaken, it was only one of many themes in *ukiyo-e* prints, which also record scenes of social and street life – pretty girls chasing fireflies, picnics, fishing parties, famous *kabuki* actors in their most celebrated roles, birds and flowers,

travellers in rain and snow, and landscapes. The most celebrated is probably Hokusai's series of views of Mount Fuji, Japan's sacred volcano, seen from different vantage points, in different weathers, and as a backdrop to varied scenes – fishermen casting their nets, travellers measuring the girth of a gigantic cryptomeria tree, the three cargo boats battling with a wild sea in that most dramatic of all Japanese prints, 'The Great Wave at Kanagawa'. Hokusai, who signed his later prints 'Gakyo-Rojin', or Old Man Mad with Painting, died in 1849 at the age of 89, having painted more than thirty thousand designs. His *One Hundred Views of Mount Fuji,* published in London in 1880, was the first comprehensive introduction to *ukiyo-e,* and made a profound impression on the rising generation of artists, notably the Impressionist school.

THE MAKING OF UKIYO-E

JAPANESE WOODBLOCK PRINTS are generally regarded as a pinnacle of achievement in this form. One reason for this is a native tradition of exquisite, painstaking craftsmanship in every branch of the applied arts – textile printing, lacquer work, ceramics, metalwork, carving in wood, ivory. To a certain extent, the production of *ukiyo-e* was a team effort, a collaboration between the publisher, the artist, the carver and the printer, and this was honoured, in some cases, by allowing all these to add their personal seals to the prints. Japanese mulberry fibre paper at this time was the finest in the world, strong but absorbent enough to take clean imprints of line and colour. The block engravers, prodigiously skilled, worked on smooth slabs of hardwood such as catalpa or cherry. The printing process began with the artist's completed drawing, in Indian ink on thin paper. This was pasted face up onto the woodblock, and the carver then went to work with special tools and gouges, cutting and scraping away all the surrounding wood through the paper to leave the line drawing in relief.

Two kabuki *actors, depicted in celebrated roles, in a delicately and typically coloured Japanese woodblock print.*

THE SPIRIT OF THE PRINTS

UKIYO-E WERE PRINTED and sold in varying formats. As well as the horizontal or vertical, corresponding to our 'landscape' and 'portrait' shapes, there were print sequences, printed as diptychs and triptychs and clearly intended to be viewed alongside each other, since the visual narrative overflows onto the next-door print. One curious development of print format was the *hashira-e,* or pillar print, long and narrow and intended to be hung on the supporting pillars of a traditional Japanese home. Their curious proportions presented a pictorial and design challenge which most artists experimented with and some, like Harunobu and his pupil Koryūsai, found so stimulating they made them their own. 'Beauties' wrapped in lavishly printed kimonos were the favourite theme, and it is thought that the increasing tendency of *ukiyo-e* artists to present their beauties as long slender creatures, further elongated by intricately piled hairdos and platform sandals, was one result of working in this format. Tall, willowy Japanese beauties, as is well known, are the exception rather than the rule, but it is normal for pin-ups to idealize their subjects, and these elegant, attenuated figures belong to a tradition as old as Greek statuary and as new as a supermodel.

However, the overall tendency of *ukiyo-e* print treatment and subject-matter was towards increasing realism: street or theatre scenes swarming with life and humour, and landscapes powerfully represented as real places subject to changing moods, due to sudden furious rainstorms, swirling mist, blanketing snow. The Japanese landscape is famously varied and picturesque, and the Japanese have an intense feeling for nature. What lingers in the mind after studying books or original prints in the genre is their startling and dramatic composition, so modern as now to seem familiar. They depict a lingering and luxurious enjoyment of beautiful detail: a printed kimono, sprays of cherry blossom, the soft blobs of falling snow. They also allude to the pervasive poetry of a race which turned unself-consciously to composing *haiku* in response to a new moon, a flight of geese or a moment of sensuous bliss.

The finished block was cleaned and inked and a sheet of mulberry paper laid over it, and then rubbed firmly on the back with a hard, round pad, *baren.* In the early days of *ukiyo-e,* before full colour printing became commonplace, many of these ink prints were sold as black-and-white, or rather cream (the mulberry paper colour) impressions. Some were hand-coloured, or stencilled. As the market for prints grew, so too did the public demand for colour, bright, intense, varied. New skill in registration, plus increasing profitability, led printers away from the gentle, limited colours, mostly rose and green, of the early coloured prints towards the spectacular polychrome of the later 'brocade prints'.

The artist associated with the first essays into full colour in the 1760s was Harunobu, whose lyrical portraits of 'beauties' in natural settings are some of the most charming and tender expressions of the *bijin-ga* tradition. Instead of the restricted palette of the earlier rose prints, these brocade prints use eight separate colours, some in several shades. This required the cutting of as many separate woodblocks, a lengthy and necessarily more expensive process.

DYESTUFFS AND PRINTED CLOTHS

A tumbled, glistening heap of raw silk yarn fresh from the dyer's vat in Marrakesh, Morocco.

Printing seems, almost certainly, to have been used first as a means of decorating cloth, for clothing or hangings or ceremonial purposes. The relative fragility of cloth means that the earliest known examples, Coptic, date from the fifth century AD, but written evidence suggests that printed, patterned cloths go back at least two thousand years in India and Egypt, and, perhaps, China. The emphasis today has shifted so far in the direction of printing as information that this might seem a little surprising, until one recollects that people must have responded to the appeal of colourful clothing long before they became literate. In other words, you don't need to be able to read and write to want to look your best.

It seems probable that tie dye was the first method used to pattern cloth, simply because the means would have been cheap and to hand, and the process is direct. Printing with wooden blocks involves designing and carving the blocks, and a more sophisticated use of mordants and resist processes. But both methods of patterning cloth depended from the outset on a knowledge of dyestuffs, and experience in handling them. How this knowledge was arrived at can only be a matter of conjecture. However, the properties of the first dyestuffs, all of vegetable origin – principally indigo, madder, saffron and, to a lesser extent, barks, roots, even the humble onion skin – seem to have been discovered locally, and independently, wherever these plants flourished. Indigo grows abundantly in both India and Africa and both countries have ancient skills and traditions in indigo-dyed patterned cloths, though Indian tradition favours tie dye and African starch-paste resist.

Indigo dyeing is unusual in that the process requires a cool or tepid dye-bath temperature, rather than the boiling needed for most dyes to penetrate and permanently stain the cloth fibres. Again, one can see how this factor must have favoured its use in areas where fuel was in short supply and dyeing cloth was of lower priority, perhaps, than cooking food.

ORGANIC DYES

Natural, organic dyestuffs derive from plants of one sort or another. The recent interest in reviving organic or vegetable dyes has led to a new appreciation of their intrinsic beauty of colour, more intense or more subtle than the colours arrived at by the modern pharmacopoeia of synthetic, chemical-based dyes. Although a synthetic indigo dye is available, it is doubtful whether it will ever supplant its organic predecessor. Vegetable dye colours are more radiant, and at the same time softer looking, and they age gracefully, fading gradually but always beautifully. Ironically, perhaps, the world-wide passion for blue jeans, originally a cheap form of industrial clothing, has probably done more than anything else to alert the public to the special appeal of an organic dye process. The recent influx of tribal rugs and kelims from the Middle East and Eastern Europe may have contributed to a growing sensitivity to the visual difference between traditional organic dyes and their harsher-looking, synthetic modern equivalents. But given the pressure of market forces, and an acceptable price point, it seems sadly inevitable that traditional dyeing processes will gradually succumb to faster, less skilled, more

Africa has its own ancient tradition of indigo tie dyeing. Here two women set out printed and dyed cloths to dry in Sierra Leone.

profitable mass-production methods, leaving the craft-based cottage industry to keep the old skills alive, offering a small but discriminating public goods coloured and patterned in the traditional way.

While organic dyes proved adequate to the needs of early cloth printing methods, such as tie dye, the introduction of block printing created a need for more complex dyeing, such as the discharge process. Here the block print is transferred onto cloth via a mordant, or fixing agent, the cloth is then dyed and the un-mordanted areas cleared of colour by subsequent bleaching, by chemical means and by the simple expedient of laying the cloth out to undergo the scouring of the weather. The un-mordanted areas could then be dyed a different colour, if this was intended in the original design. The mordant, varying from one dyestuff to another, and within one dyestuff (like madder, which yields colours from pink and lilac through red or purple to nearly black) depending on what colours were wanted, creates insoluble coloured

areas. The name derives from the French *mordre,* to bite, and the aim is to effect a chemical union between the cloth fibres and the colour which will survive washing, light, and so on, not to mention the fierce discharge process itself. It remains mysterious, to a lay mind, that a piece of cloth can be subjected to so many stringent chemical processes and emerge gloriously coloured and patterned, smooth and resilient, and able to survive a long life of wear and tear. Undoubtedly, natural fibres – wool, silk, cotton – stand up best to this initial assault, whether by boiling, bleaching, burnishing with smooth stones, or any of the other tricks used to produce a printed cloth of irresistible appeal.

The challenge facing dyers from the beginning was to extend their colour range. Though this could be done, to a limited extent, by combining different mordants with a particular vegetable dye, madder in particular, the quest for greater variety was keen and led in time to the use of so-called mineral colours – antimony orange, Prussian blue, manganese brown. Both these and the vegetable dyestuffs were used in combination with a wide variety of mordants to deliver different shades. Mordants, commonly known as 'drugs' in the eighteenth century, divided into two categories: 'true mordants', metallic salts – alum, tin, iron, copper – whose oxides effected a chemical union between the cloth fibres and the colouring matter in question; and the 'not true mordants' – oils, albumen, casein – which act quite differently, binding the colouring agent to the fibres mechanically, like a glue, rather than fusing it through the fibres like a stain or dye. Both processes were known and practised quite early on in the history of cloth printing. The Indian palampores, or painted cloths, which dazzled European fashionables from the seventeenth century onwards, traditionally combined dyeing techniques with final, hand-painted touches of colour not then achievable – or not easily or cheaply – through standard dyeing processes.

Indian palampores of this period remain unsurpassed in their delicate beauty of design and freshness of colouring. They are products of an ancient skill and knowledge, as well as artistry, which did more than anything else to sharpen imitation and competition in Europe, crudely at first, but with increasing commercial acumen. European versions, of more or less sensitivity, began to supersede the

Courtiers at the Kraton Palace, Jakarta, Java, wearing traditional batik-printed sarongs and turbans.

originals in the marketplace, relying on technological advances in printing to produce exotically patterned cloth at an affordable price, which few people were in a position to compare with costly imported palampores to their disadvantage. In time this led to the development of printed cloths, like the celebrated *toile de Jouy*, whose witty and charming *camaieu* (or cameo) designs, in monochrome against a white ground, became the most fashionable patterned fabrics for both clothing and furnishing in mid-eighteenth-century France. Palampores are now collectors' items, but *toile de Jouy* is still being manufactured, and has become a classic option for interior decorators seeking charm, elegance and freshness of colouring.

Though cloth printing and paper printing technology occasionally overlapped over the centuries – one instance is the use of intaglio printing for *toile de Jouy* – the two industries seem, on the whole, to have developed quite separately. Fabric printing lagged behind in terms of mass-production until the nineteenth century, when various innovations, notably aniline dyes and roller printing machinery, brought it into a new, burgeoning and immensely profitable marketplace.

Yarns tie dyed for ikat *weaving drying on washing lines in Kathmandu, Nepal.*

SYNTHETIC DYES

ANILINE, OR SYNTHETIC, DYESTUFFS, originally a by-product of coal tar, began with an eighteen-year-old research assistant, William Henry Perkins, playing about in his laboratory during the Easter holidays in a vague attempt to synthesize quinine, at that time the only known anti-malarial drug. In the course of his experiments, young William Henry observed that the black, tarry substance he had isolated contained a coloured precipitate, which he subsequently christened 'mauveine' and which, when worn by Queen Victoria in the shape of a dyed silk crinoline, became the flavour of that month, and many more. It led in a few years to Magenta, named after a recent victory in the Crimean War, and to Alizarin crimson, based on the colouring matter of madder, and artificially reproduced by the German chemists Graebe and Liebermann. The new synthetic dyes inaugurated a crude rush of colour in fabric printing. Almost overnight, it seems, all is cacophony instead of harmony. Vividness and violent contrast, magenta with canary yellow or pea green, is all the rage. Aniline dyes were less appealing, aesthetically, but they were simpler to use at a critical juncture in the fabric printing industry, when mass-production methods, such as roller printing, were transforming the production of printed textiles.

Roller printing borrowed from intaglio printing techniques, using acid etching processes to transfer a textile design to a roller made of a thick layer of copper over a steel core. Subsequently, chrome plating the roller increased its print capacity by several hundred thousand yards. This was pretty near to being a fully automated process, and allowed textile manufacture to become a seriously profitable line of business for such figures as Robert Peel, future British Prime Minister, one of the first to come from a 'trade' background.

THE ROMANCE OF TEXTILES

INEVITABLY, THESE TECHNICAL ADVANCES gave rise to a backlash, as romantic idealists like William Morris recognized the threat they posed to the integrity and beauty of traditional hand-printed textiles, coloured with organic dyes, which had been developed with such skill and traditional wisdom over previous centuries all over the world. With typical energy and enthusiasm, Morris re-invented the wheel, metaphorically speaking, tracking down one man, Thomas Wardle of Leek, who still remembered how patterned and printed cloth was produced in his boyhood using woodblocks, discharge processes and organic dyestuffs like madder and indigo.

Unquestionably Morris was one of the great pattern-makers, or designers, of all time, and his magnificently intricate, subtle yet vividly fresh designs, hand-blocked on linen, velveteen and other textiles, remain a benchmark and inspiration to individual designers and to the trade in general even a century and a half later. But just as importantly, he had the vision, taste and

Colourful as a bed of zinnias, synthetic and natural dyestuffs mingle in flamboyant saris worn at the festival of the Carpenter God in Rajasthan, India.

23

doggedness needed to rediscover, test and perfect, to an extent exploiting recent technology, the use of the oldest, simplest, and still most beautiful of all dyestuffs, and the most labour intensive yet unsurpassed fabric printing techniques, for translating his designs onto a printed cloth.

DECORATIVE PRINTED PAPERS

T HOUGH THERE IS A TENDENCY today to assume that printing proper began with Gutenberg, since with hindsight it seems incontrovertible that the invention of letterpress was a watershed in human history, the facts are somewhat different. Block printing for decorative, even frivolous, purposes was well-established in Europe several centuries before the invention of moveable type. Block-printed textiles were produced in the Rhineland from early medieval times, printed playing cards, crude but relieved by dabs of hand-applied colour, were in general circulation, and block-printed decorative papers, on small sheets, and usually imitating wood grain effects, have been found on the ceilings, infilling timber compartments, of German castles of the early fifteenth century. Though Northern Europe, particularly Germany and Holland, made conspicuous use of these *faux* papers, the centre for manufacture of decorative papers seems to have been Italy, a tradition which has survived with the famous patterned and marbled 'Florentine' papers up to the present day.

What our ancestors wanted, it is clear, was pattern, colour and, to some extent, recognizable images reflecting the world as they knew it. The earliest surviving pictorial print, known as the 'tapestry of Sion', a mural hanging printed in oil colours on linen, was produced in Venice in the late fourteenth century.

Relief-printed playing cards, sometimes stencilled in colour, were one of the first examples of decorative printing in Europe. This block, dating from the seventeenth century, is incredibly finely detailed.

There is some evidence that decorative printed papers, borders, loose sheets, and 'paste-on' ornaments for furniture were already quite sophisticated by Gutenberg's time, and achieved a level of design and production which book illustration, with its crude black-and-white woodcuts, was not to match for several centuries.

The notion of printed papers being a poor man's facsimile of a costly material – hardwood, marble, marquetry – seems to have been important from the beginning, and indeed has remained an added attraction of the more lavish wallpapers right down to the present day. Printed paper borders simulating complicated marquetry inlays were already popular in the fifteenth century, pasted onto solid but provincial pieces of furniture and varnished heavily to resemble fashionable inlaid ornament, in different coloured wood. Later, oriental lacquerware became a coveted status symbol throughout Europe. Italian printers turned out coloured printed sheets of motifs in the bizarre, or chinoiserie mode, which were stuck down onto gaily painted furniture and highly varnished, and became known as 'Japan' work.

BEFORE 1700

PRINTED, PATTERNED SHEETS, sold loose (this was long before printed paper could be sold in continuous rolls) were popular from the sixteenth century, and were bought to line boxes and chests, as book endpapers, and increasingly to hang, pasted side by side, as wallpaper. In France, which led the market in terms of design, colour and variety in the seventeenth century, these were known as *papiers dominos*, and the street vendor of them, shown in a contemporary print as a saucy young woman with a skirt made up of variegated papers, overlapped like flower petals, was known as a *dominotière*. Every sheet displays a different design – spots, chevrons, stripes, flowers in the most brilliant colours. In the background, the production of *papiers dominos* is recorded, one man and two women busying about a large printing table.

The *papiers dominos* seem to be the provincial version of the grander *papiers de tapisserie* introduced in the early eighteenth century. Jean Michel Papillon, son of a wallpaper maker and descendent of a long line of print-makers, published an illustrated book on wood engraving and woodblock printing in the eighteenth century in which he pours scorn on the *papiers dominos*: 'all dominos are without taste, poorly drawn, even worse coloured and stencilled with harsh colours'. In contrast, the *papiers de tapisserie* were closely printed with designs of filigree delicacy, and hand coloured. Also, due to a new invention, counter-proofing, where a freshly printed sheet was pressed against a plain sheet to create its mirror image, a design could be extended

further than the confines of the standard sheet 18 x 20 inches (45 x 50 cm) in size. Standards of execution aside, both types of *papiers* were still produced in single sheets, and the methods of printing and colouring them appear identical.

Woodblocks carved with the design were fastened face up to the printing table. Colour (printing ink at first, but later distemper) was dabbed over the block, the sheet of paper laid on top and the design printed off by rolling a padded roller across the top. Once the inked design was dry, extra colour was brushed on either freehand or through a stencil. In the earlier papers, the colour is quite transparent, presumably so as not to mask the printed detail. Later in the eighteenth century, when distemper colours were preferred for decorative papers because of their richer texture and opacity, the stencilled colours were often applied first, one stencil to each colour, and the block printing, which supplied outline and detail, superimposed in a contrasting colour, or black.

The designs of these seventeenth-century decorative papers stem from many sources – Renaissance pattern books, embroidery and lace-working manuals, woven tapestry and fashionable printed or woven textiles. Despite the difficulty of printing and assembling a wallpaper imitating tapestry out of dozens of separate sheets, one or two French examples survive from the mid-eighteenth century. These would definitely have been *papiers de tapisseries*, not *dominos*, which never attempted anything more complicated than a small, vivid, overall repeat pattern. However, it must be said that the simple gaiety of the *dominos* papers, with their sprigs and stripes, is more appealing to a modern eye than the somewhat pretentious and over-worked designs of the *papiers de tapisserie*.

By the late seventeenth century, another distinctive category of printed decorative papers was gaining in popularity. Marbled papers, created in a variety of designs by floating colours mixed with ox-gall on a bed of liquid or gelatine (carrageen moss was often used for this) and combing or spotting them before laying sheets of paper on top, were a fashionable oddity, often used to fill overmantel panels for a grand effect, rather as painted marbling might be used today. *Papiers brillants*, or sparkling papers, were made by block printing paper with fish glue or size and sprinkling over crushed mica or metallic powders. The market for these novelty papers was limited, but the *papiers brillants* must have influenced the techniques used during the eighteenth century to mimic cut velvets, brocade and damask.

THE EIGHTEENTH CENTURY

DURING THE EIGHTEENTH CENTURY, England seems to have overtaken the rest of Europe in the production of stylish printed papers, their designs and colouring closely modelled on the sumptuous silk and velvet textiles used to line the upper walls (above the dado) of the more important, state rooms of aristocratic houses. A new class of wealthy, but not outlandishly rich, socially mobile and ambitious entrepreneurs and self-made men, like Samuel Pepys, admired and coveted the glamour and opulence of the stately-home decor. Recognizing what we would call a 'gap in the market', English paper printers rapidly evolved a cut-price version, producing papers imitative of cut velvets and brocades of such excellence that they could only with difficulty have been identified as a 'poor man's' imitation. Ironically, many of these have survived, in splendid repair, long after the originals have gone the way of the most expensive fibres, fading, 'perishing' or, in the case of silk, 'cutting' till the merest ghost is left of their original splendour.

'Flocking', where cut fibres are attached to a design printed with glue on variously treated grounds – distemper painted, varnished for lustre, overall printed with a tiny diaper motif – was the wallpaper finish of choice in England in the early eighteenth century, and in America for another fifty years. Many examples survive, testifying to their astonishing durability, notably a magnificent baroque pomegranate design hung at Clandon Park, Surrey, a rococo floral design on a mica ground in the Sarah Orne Jewitt House in South Berwick, Maine, and a superbly vivid pink ground paper flocked in crimson in the drawing room at Lydiard Park, Wiltshire. The colourfulness and opulence of these papers would have recommended them to a discerning eye, especially when word got round that their cost was a fraction, a third to a sixth, of the cost of the fabrics they imitated. The patterns used for most of the grander flock wallpapers, a British speciality at the time, are straight steals from the formal, stylized fruit and flower motifs of the baroque damasks, cut velvets and brocades, themselves distantly derived from earlier Ottoman textiles and embroideries.

Splendid as these papers are, they would have proved overwhelming in scale in the smaller, lower-ceilinged rooms of the gentry and aspiring bourgeoisie. Perhaps the most delightful papers of the period are in the modest but special category, like a particularly charming, vivid, floral paper rescued from a house in Burford, Oxfordshire, stencilled in pale pink flowers and tendrils on a vivid yellow ground and block printed over in sharp puce. The colour combination is daring, but perfectly judged, delivering the sort of visual charge found in some Indian textiles. Small-scale diaper patterns in quieter shades of blue, with matching borders, also survive, looking strangely contemporary but probably reflecting a growing taste for small and simple overall designs on calicoes, then a portmanteau word for any type of printed or patterned cotton cloth.

It should be noted that the papers used in the production of all these early eighteenth-century designs were still manufactured in the single sheet form, and then pasted together to make continuous lengths, an English innovation. The intricate over-printing would have disguised this underlying patchwork, helped by the fact that most paper 'hangings' were mounted on stretched canvas, which provided an ideally taut, smooth base.

But the design influence which probably did more than anything to galvanize decorative paper-making in the latter part of the century was altogether exotic. It came from India, first, in the shape of hand-painted and printed chintzes, or palampores, and secondly, from China, in the form of hand-painted wallpapers, showing birds, flowers and foliage, executed in brilliant gouache colours on a white mulberry-type paper called *mien lien*. Here, instead of the sober grandeur of the

sumptuous brocade hangings and their flock-printed imitations, was fantasy, a dazzling but exquisitely rendered landscape of dreams. Anyone who could afford them longed to transform a boudoir or bedroom into a fantastical scene from Cathay, peopled with men in pointed hats, or oval-faced beauties in flowing robes, promenading through a stylized landscape.

All Chinese papers were hand painted, and expensive, but English paper hangers were quick to supply their own, home-grown and considerably cheaper papers in the same idiom. A few of these 'pastiche' papers survive, faded and discoloured compared with the Chinese papers, but finally no more than a distant and heavy-handed echo of a world which any eighteenth-century printer or paper-maker would have found too outlandish to be credible.

But the vivid colour, asymmetrical design and airy pale backgrounds seen in both Indian chintz and Chinese wallpaper designs became an important influence on the printed papers, or *papiers peints,* which dominated fashionable interior decoration throughout both Europe and America in the late eighteenth and early nineteenth centuries. This was a period when wallpaper was so much the accepted mark of social status and civilized society that American itinerant stencillers travelled New England on commission to transform austerely-painted boarded walls with clambering floral motifs, in orderly stripes, drawn from the pattern books of European wallpaper manufacturers.

THE NINETEENTH CENTURY AND BEYOND

TECHNICALLY, early nineteenth-century papers were superb, masterful in design, lavish in their colouring, provided with *en suite* borders and friezes. Floral designs remained the most popular, as ever, but there was a new vogue for wallpapers imitating elaborately draped textiles, rendered with awesome verisimilitude. This had its origins in neo-classicism, when softly folded and gathered muslins, reminiscent of Greek statuary drapery, were fashionable. But the earlier cult

'The Bedroom at Langton Hall', Yorkshire, painted by Mary Ellen Best in 1835. This delightful room shows block-printed wallpaper almost certainly harking back in design to the late eighteenth century.

of simplicity and purity was rapidly superseded as rival companies vied to create showier and more dazzling effects, culminating in the astonishing paper representing transparent flounces of embroidered net which won the Swiss firm of Zuber two gold medals in the 1830s. The ravishing delicacy of the printing was made possible by Zuber's use of engraved copper cylinders from 1826, one of the first examples of contemporary advances in printing techniques in other fields, such as book illustrations and fabric printing, being employed in the hitherto conservative printed paper industry. Wallpapers were quick to reflect new fashions in interior decoration. A *coup de théâtre* in design terms was the scenic wallpaper, showing a panorama made up of many 'drops' that required expert hanging, but allowed the wealthy bourgeoisie to emulate the mural paintings that decorated aristocratic homes. Most of these were by Zuber, and are eagerly collected today for their decorative impact and as triumphs of nineteenth-century printing.

It must be said, however, that as wallpaper printers became more adept and technically skilful, the result tended toward a showiness that often lapsed into vulgarity and distracting fussiness. These were not 'background' papers, discreetly patterned and coloured, against which paintings and family portraits, or framed prints, would show to advantage. Flamboyant, often coloured in combinations which set the teeth on edge, they simply took over a room, with an 'in your face' display of wealth and uncertain taste. One can imagine them appealing to Dickens's parodic *nouveau riche* couple, the Veneerings.

Inevitably, as the century advanced, there was a reaction. It led in England to the establishment of Morris and Co. William Morris, drawing on varied influences, from medieval illumination, antique tapestry and embroidery to Iznik ceramics, created designs for his company which were satisfyingly complex, but not fussy: mostly of plants and flowers, stylized but directly observed and springy with life. He printed them in subtle colour combinations which manage to be at once rich and subdued. They were block printed in distemper colours, for the matt, velvety texture which distinguishes this paint. They are still printed today, though some of the mass-produced patterns have been re-coloured unsatisfactorily, with an inevitable loss of vitality. Nevertheless, his much loved Willow Bough design, in its mass-market version,

'Let Us Prey' watercolour master design for a Voysey wallpaper of the late nineteenth century. C. F. Voysey (1857-1941) succeeded Morris as a designer in the Arts and Crafts tradition.

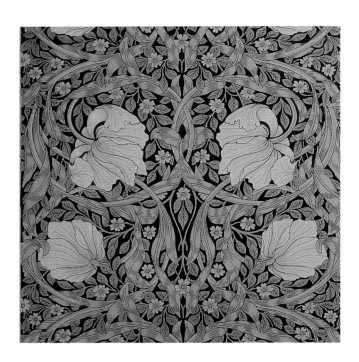

'Pimpernel', one of the less familiar wallpaper designs by William Morris, shows his characteristic swirling plant forms allied to sensitive, hand-blocked colour.

remains one of the most refreshing and beautiful interior complements to the English landscape outside.

The twentieth century has seen an explosion of cheap, mass-market printed wallpapers, mostly of inferior design and muddy colouring. However, there have been artists who experimented with designing in this field, including such inter-war names as Edward Bawden and Graham Sutherland, and their work has a wit and liveliness that makes one wish their work could be reprinted. A few enthusiasts undertake commissions for hand-blocked wallpapers – not cheap, but less expensive than the showier commercial papers. It is ironic, with mass-production printing techniques at such a high level of sophistication, that there is a growing interest in the traditional, hand-blocked item. One reason may well be the mass-market pre-dilection for vinyl-treated, washable papers, which have an unpleasantly plastic texture. This devalues any design, however faithfully and cleverly it is printed, and encourages the imaginative and enterprising to take matters into their own hands.

PRINTING
PROJECTS

TOOLS

There is something irresistibly purposeful, honed by use and tradition, about a collection of tools of the trade. It remains an area where wooden handles are still preferred to plastic, and resilient natural bristle to synthetic fibres. Quality stuff, in other words.

Reading clockwise from top centre: a radiator roller, small and deft, and best for rolling emulsion (latex) paints onto a block, then a length of dowel, improvised rolling pin for clay, and a pair of wooden tongs. Wooden spoons are invaluable for mixing dyes, etc. Round-topped bristle stencil brush, now the favourite with stencillers. Lino-cutting tools, 'U'- and 'V'-shaped gouges, are basic lino-cutting equipment. Sharp scissors are a must. A silk screen frame, and squeegee, are needed if you plan to screen fabrics. A handsome Japanese paint brush, in bamboo handle, and *djanting*, (*see* page 73) will start you off on batik work. A small rubber lino-block roller is best for taking oil-based inks. The contraption in the bottom left is a wax pot for keeping melted wax at a steady temperature, useful if you are taking batik seriously. Artists' brushes, flat, pointed, bushy, in various sizes and real bristle are a seriously worthwhile investment. Sharp pencils, essential for most projects. Palette knives, whippy and slim, are delicious tools; you can use them for filling furniture, modelling, too. A clutch of tiny tie-dye extras next: chick peas, a roll of soft wire, paper clips. And lastly three basic pieces of equipment: boxwood ruler (steel is fine), scalpel (keep lots of spare blades handy) and a good set-square for making sure that all right angles really are 90°, or your whole design effort could slide into the surreal.

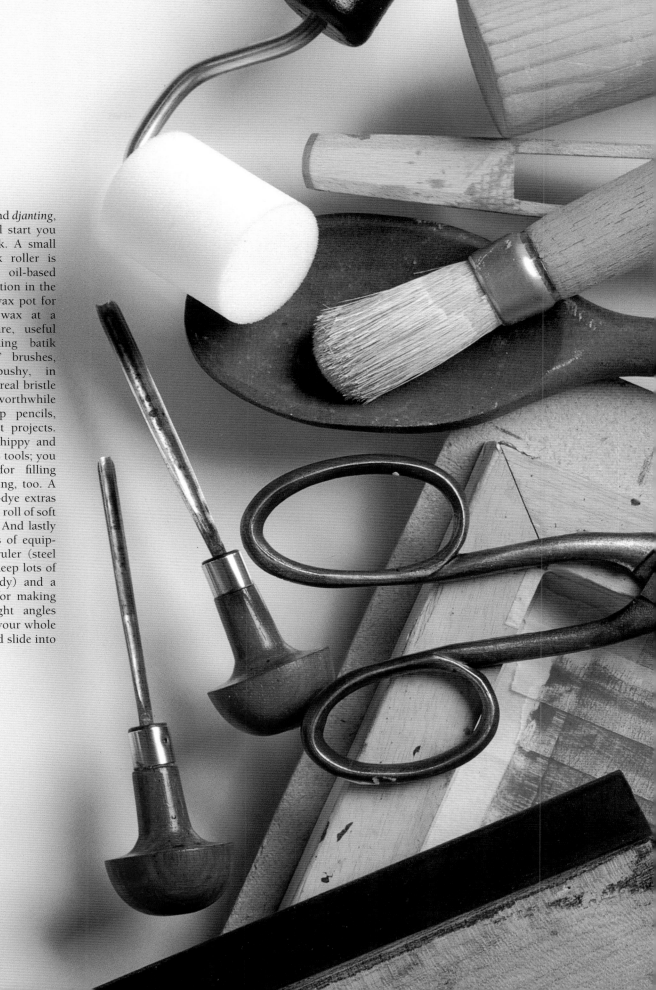

MATERIALS

This is a line-up of specific equipment, from fabrics to coils of rope and upholstery foam, required for projects in this book. We are into resourcefulness and lateral thinking here – found objects, balsa wood blocks, the model-maker's favourite, even the humble spud – all of which play a starring role in one shape or form in this book.

Reading clockwise from top centre: fabrics, calico, silk, well-washed to remove dressing, and prinked up with paper clips, etc., for dyeing. Silk screen frame, for rapid printing. Found letter blocks. Balsa wood, easy to cut as cheese, for instant printing blocks. Spirally shapes of stiff wire for fast batik work, and beneath them lino blocks, cut and uncut, with a gouge. A fat eraser is the raw material for

your own rubber stamp, and next to it, the modest potato, capable of great flights of decorative fancy. Happenstance materials, or 'found printing materials' next – a coil of rope, a spool of draught excluder tape. Beneath these, the invaluable oiled manila stencil card. A handful of nuts made a deep impression on our nutty frame. Lastly, two handy materials, one ancient – modelling clay – one more or less high-tech – upholsterer's foam – which we used to carve decorative stamps.

This is just the sort of random kit which our projects necessitated. They are intended to set your mind working laterally. They are not definitive, by any means. Half the fun of trying out ideas illustrated here is finding they spark off inventions of your own.

MEDIA

Without doubt, the advent of acrylic water-based printing inks and paints have made life a lot easier for decorative print-makers, especially screen printers, who are now able to clean up their screens after each colour printing far more rapidly and less messily than in the past. Screen printing inks specifically made for the purpose are the ones to go for, sold in many colours and various sizes. Standard emulsion (latex) paints give exceptional coverage and can be used for quite a few projects in the book. They come in a huge range of colours and can usually be bought in sample jar size.

Reading clockwise from top centre: a jar contains Frosting Medium (*see* p. 191), which we used for our

'etched' window. Next is a tin of blue oil-based block-printing ink; then a small jar continng red fabric paint. The spoon points out three powder fabric dyes used in tie dyeing and batik. The small jar with dropper is a ready-mixed watercolour, and the three small tubes are water-based printing inks for block printing. Ink pads come next, for use with rubber stamps, homemade or ready-to-go. The small, hexagonal jars are stencil paints, available in sixteen colours including gold, silver and pewter. The orange jar contains silk screen ink. The small jars with white lids above are acrylic enamels, Glossies (*see* p. 191), used in the book for ceramic painting. Above these, the two different tubes are artists' water-based paints: acrylic and gouache, often used to tint emulsion paint, as well as on their own. Finally, a sheet of silver leaf (aluminium transfer leaf is cheaper and easier for beginners to use) with a spoonful of Japan Gold size in the saucer on top.

POTATOCUTS

As PRINTING TOOLS GO, the potato cut is something of a blunt instrument, restricted as to size and intolerant of fine detail. Its playschool associations tell against it too, though I still treasure a rather elegant little abstract, in three colours, which my eldest daughter, aged six, shrugged off in that casually confident way of young children, without a moment's thought or hesitation. And raising the stakes, do not forget what Matisse created with that other playschool standby, coloured paper, scissors and paste.

Understanding the limitations of the material while exploiting its possibilities is the challenge and satisfaction of print making, in whatever medium. With care and finesse, the humble carved spud can be made to yield effects well outside the scope of little, impatient fingers. Adult hands have learned control; we can be trusted with sharp scalpels; and we can supply ourselves with finer materials than poster colours and sugar paper.

But first, why potatoes? Why not parsnips, celeriac, swedes or other tubers? Firstly, potatoes are cheap and you can find them anywhere. But, more specifically, potatoes have a waxy rather than fibrous consistency which makes them fairly easy to cut and carve cleanly. Secondly, potatoes are full of starch, a natural glue, which gives body and 'stick' to your potato prints. Thirdly, a cut potato can be stored overnight in cold water without significant softening or deterioration. All in all, a handy vegetable.

Recent technology has had a helpful input too. Playschool colours are cheap but

37

not 'fast' – they wash off, smudge and give blurry prints. Acrylic colours, though water based, dry fast in both senses of the word – quickly and unbudgeably, to the extent that acrylic-based prints on fabric can even be washed, albeit carefully and preferably by hand. Alternatively, PVA (polyvinyl acetate), a bonding agent with innumerable uses, can be added to coloured inks to ensure fastness.

If all this sounds alarmingly technical or complicated, you will be reassured to learn that a very satisfactory paint for potato printing can be made up from a mix of emulsion (latex) paint (which contains acrylic), wallpaper paste and a little water. The wallpaper paste, together with the natural potato starch, adds crispness to prints and the effect of greater transparency of colour – all of which creates variety and liveliness in the final result.

A last note about technique. Inevitably, there is a tendency to think of potato cuts as stamps to be plonked onto the colour and then plonked onto the surface to be decorated. We are all conditioned by distant memories of rubber stamping – at passport control, perhaps – to see the stamping action as a simple, two-step technique. This remains, undoubtedly, the great underlying appeal of the huge success of rubber stamps as decorative tools (*see* p. 55). Experience has shown that this approach is unsuited to most other printing tools. It picks up colour in a hit-and-miss way, too much or too little, or unevenly, all deleterious to the clean, crisp, controlled image wanted. To achieve this, colour in whatever form is best applied to the stamp by roller or brush. This way you can soon anticipate, to a nicety, the clarity, depth of colour or transparency of the resulting print. Otherwise the print will be something between a splat and a smudge and we are back at playschool.

THE TECHNIQUE

POTATO CUT MOTIFS are best kept simple but shapely. Their size is obviously determined by that of the potato, so keep a selection to hand. The basic processes involved in drawing, cutting and applying potato cuts are the same, whatever the project.

YOU WILL NEED

Potatoes
Large, sharp kitchen knife
Felt pen/sable brush
Soft, square-ended artist's brush and/or small
    roller
Scalpel, plus spare blades
Artists' acrylic colours or coloured inks or
    emulsion (latex) mixed with wallpaper paste
PVA
Lino cutting tools for cutting details/ 'U'- and
    'V'- shaped small gouges

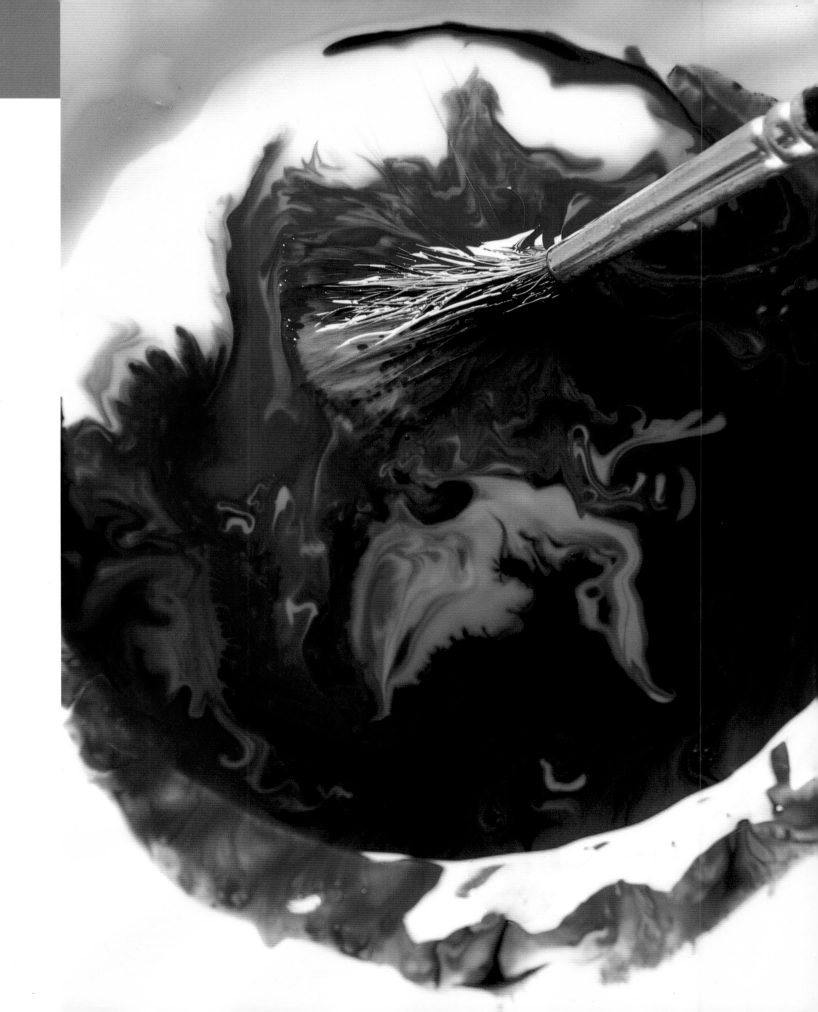

1 At the risk of stating the obvious, how you cut the potato in two is critical, because both surfaces must be absolutely flat. Arrange the potato so that it won't wobble, then cut through in one decisive stroke.

2 Press the potato firmly onto a piece of kitchen towel to remove excess moisture. The damp impression that the potato makes on the towel will also show whether or not it has been cut successfully flat.

3 Sketch out a few suitable motifs to refer to. A felt pen is handy for marking out the motif on the cut potato surface. Here, the circle and centre spot will be cut out using a lino cutting gouge.

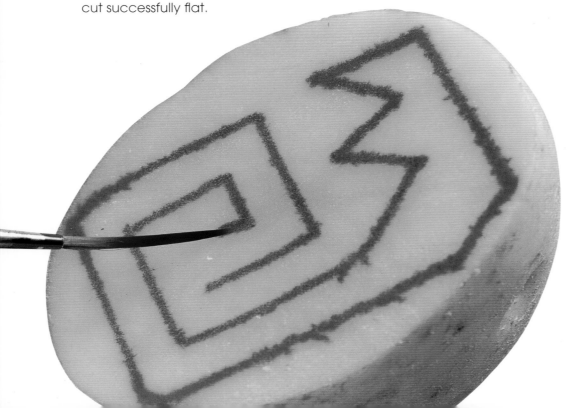

4 Some people prefer to use a fine sable brush and coloured ink to mark out their motif.

5 Once the motif is marked out, you can either cut it out as is, or brush colour over the whole surface, using a soft artist's brush, as here. This makes cutting easier, because the motif stands out more clearly.

6 The way you cut is important. Using the scalpel first, cut around your motif, angling the blade slightly to give a bevelled edge. Try not to undercut, because this weakens the stamp in use. Then use the scalpel to cut across from the perimeter to the outline cut.

7 A small 'V'-shaped gouge is useful for cutting details, like the veining of a leaf. Hold the potato firmly and gouge as smoothly as possible. You can practise this first on another potato. Use light but firm pressure in one continuous movement.

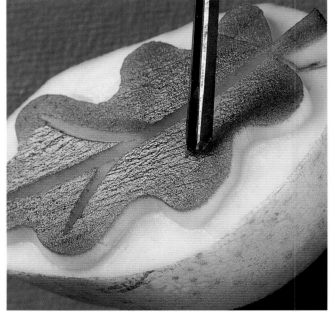

A STAMPED
ROOM BORDER

A HAND-PRINTED BORDER looks both classy and charming and costs next to nothing if you print onto strips of lining paper, which is not only cheap and metres long, but also has a useful absorbency not always found in more expensive paper. It tends to discolour a little in time, but pleasantly, to a parchment shade. If this does not appeal, varnish before pasting with a matt acrylic varnish, which will also give your border more substance and make it easier to handle when wet. Americans often combine paper borders with painted walls, a sensible policy that allows the ease of application of paint yet the decorative impact of a border, although here we have pasted our border over a papered wall.

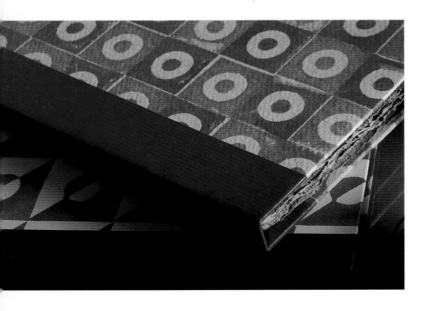

YOU WILL NEED

A roll of lining paper, cut into manageable lengths
Long, sharp scissors
Pencil/steel rule for marking out border
Potato cut/s (we used twin cuts, one for each colour)
Blue and yellow colours in one of the mixtures described on p. 38.
PVA solution

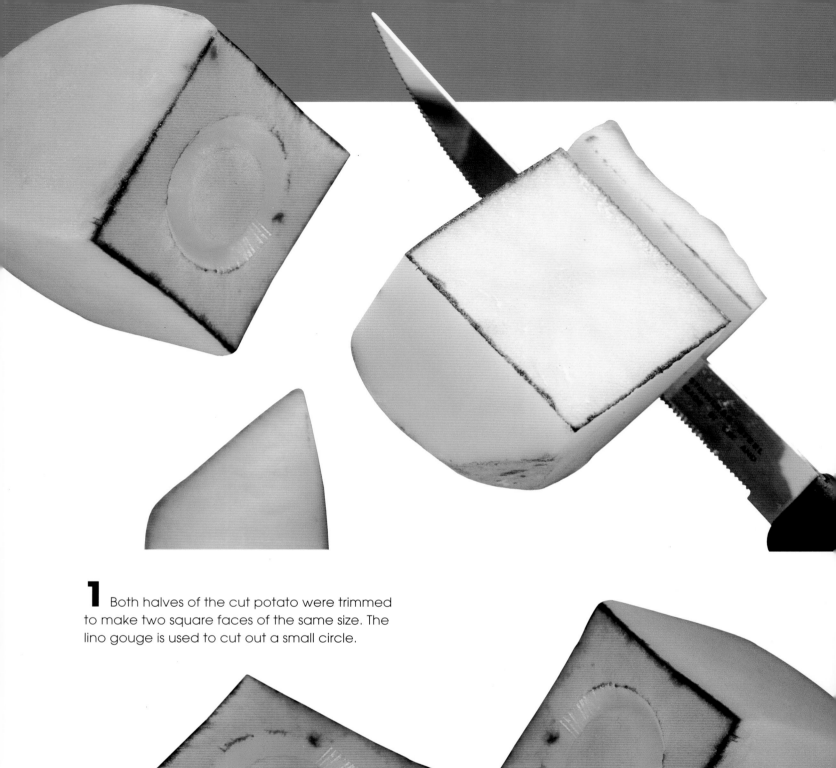

1 Both halves of the cut potato were trimmed to make two square faces of the same size. The lino gouge is used to cut out a small circle.

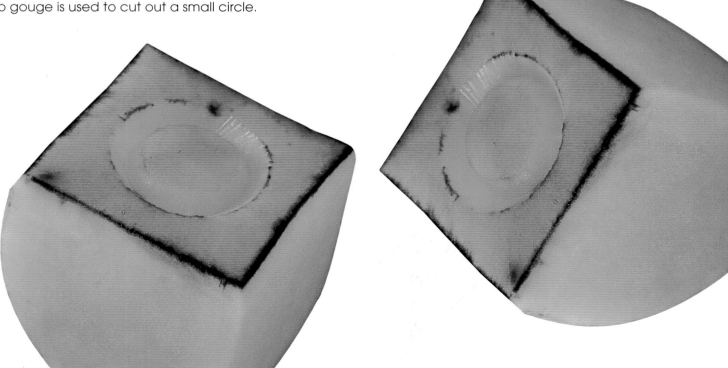

2 The stamps are used in alternation – yellow, blue, yellow – to make a simple but effective border, following pencil lines ruled the length of the lining paper. Use brush or roller to apply fresh colour every two or three prints, sparingly.

3 It is a sensible precaution to brush a dilute PVA solution over the coloured face of the border, before or after cutting, to stiffen the paper slightly and avoid the risk of smudging when wallpaper paste is applied to the back.

4 Use the long-bladed scissors to separate the stamped strips to make up a border, in preparation for pasting it to the wall.

LADDER-STAMPED
PILLOWCASE

YOU WILL NEED

Large potato
Fabric medium to make colour permanent and
   washable
Acrylic artists' colour in blue
Roller or brush for applying colour
Large sheet of thin card to back fabric while
   stamping

1 Mix the acrylic colour with fabric medium on
a waxed paper plate or small sheet of glass.
Test the mixture on paper to judge consistency
and colour.

2 Brush (or roll) colour over the motif. We used a large potato and cut a ladder shape.

3 Lay fabric over a sheet of card to absorb colour that goes through to the back. Newspaper can be used instead, but the print may leave the fabric grubby.

4 Stamp the motif onto the fabric. For solid colour, brush more paint on each time. For contrast, try using the stamp more than once to give a mixture of crisp and soft prints. We stamped the motif every which way.

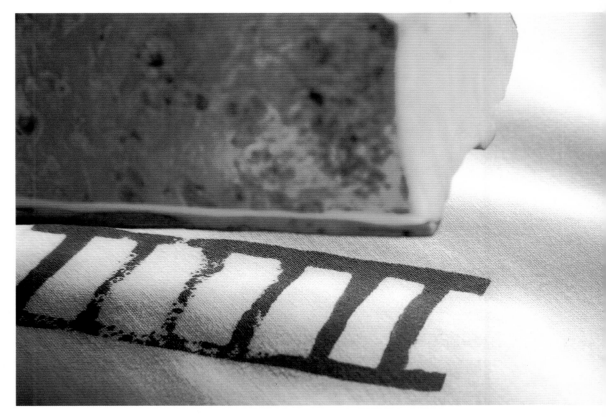

5 Follow instructions on the fabric medium for stabilizing colour to make the fabric washable – such as ironing on the back when dry.

49

A PRINTED
CURTAIN

P OTATO CUTS make very satisfactory fabric printing blocks, even for working on a large scale, as we did with these colourful curtains. They only took two hours to print. We used a yellow cotton, washed first to remove the manufacturer's stiffening, which could stop the printing ink penetrating the cloth. There are several approaches to getting stripes straight and equally spaced. I often use the edge of a long table as a guideline, with tacks each end to hold the fabric steady. Pencilled lines are another possibility or, as here, printing up to the edge of a long ruler or wooden baton. Use plenty of newspaper padding underneath to blot up excess ink. If you do want to carry on printing the next day, the potato cut can be stored overnight in a jar of clean water in the fridge. Clean off as much ink as possible first.

YOU WILL NEED

Water-based fabric printing ink (here blue, turquoise and magenta)
Small roller
Old ceramic plate as palette
Stiff artist's brush and/or palette knife
Potato cut

1 Printing inks are squeezed out onto the plate. It is impossible to measure out proportions exactly with tube colours, but make a note of roughly how much tube colour was used. Slight variations are hardly noticeable over a fabric length.

2 Use a palette knife or a stiff brush to mix the different colours thoroughly on the plate. An artist's brush does this most efficiently.

3 Use a small roller to apply colour to the potato cut before each print. Apply sparingly but evenly.

4 Use a straight edge to act as a guide when printing the stripes. Don't worry about tiny gaps between prints, as here, which are attractive evidence of hand printing.

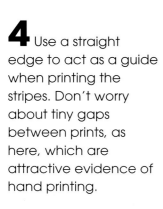

RUBBERSTAMPS

RUBBER STAMPS USED TO BE associated with officialdom, rapidly executed visual proof that your passport, visa or other documents were in order. Then the idea was borrowed for heading up stationery, and for date stamping. From there it was only a step to exploring the decorative possibilities of a rubber stamp, and the market was soon flooded with cute images of leaves, chickens, flowers and so forth, with a choice of coloured ink pads. Effective as these can be, they work best on paper. We thought it would be interesting to take the idea further, stamping a variety of different surfaces and cutting our own rubber stamps from, you guessed it, erasers in different sizes. Rubber is not the easiest material to cut, so keep to simple designs, with few curves.

The advantage of hand-cut rubber stamps is that you can cut the image in greater relief, which in turn makes it suitable for use with thicker substances than printing ink. Commercial rubber stamps, for instance, barely register on fabric. Our one use of 'found' stamps here is a set of old blocks with numbers and the alphabet, which seemed too attractive to ignore. We used them on a perfectly flat, painted wooden surface on which an adequate impression could be made by their low relief. In the other projects, our homemade stamps proved much more versatile.

The notion of making one's personal mark on documents of importance must derive from the practice of impressing carved seals onto hot wax, with the difference that on seals the design is carved out of the seal, in *intaglio*, to create a raised image on the wax. Examples of these, often carved from semi-precious stones and of exquisite workmanship, can be found in museums and date back as far as classical times. Many, though not all, are set into rings, making them conveniently to hand as well as decorative.

The ancient carved seals seem to be decorative rather than heraldic, showing mythical beasts, classical deities, lyres and other small emblems, which may have been associated with patrician families. They rarely include lettering, due to the difficulty of carving these in miniature out of hard materials. When seals were required to incorporate lettering, as with the Great Seals of State used by the English monarchs, these would have been cast in bronze.

Antique seals are eagerly collected, and expensive. But there is another, more affordable, way to appreciate the beauty and delicacy of some of these miniature carvings, and that is via replicas impressed into plaster wafers. Collections of these, probably amassed on Grand Tours during the late eighteenth-century craze for classical archaeology and generally displayed grouped in frames for hanging on a library wall, turn up quite frequently in antique shops. Authentic early examples are rare because their decorativeness makes them immediately appealing, but, inevitably, reproduction 'sets' are now available, and these are worth considering where the workmanship is adequate to the delicacy and detail of the originals. Sometimes, too, the replicas turn up singly in junk shops and these are perfect for snapping up as the start of a collection of your own.

Not a great deal of basic equipment is needed for our first project, which makes use of 'found' rubber number blocks. The blocks of all the letters of the alphabet would be equally attractive, or you could even use question marks, asterisks and other printers' devices. As the projects get more complex, the requirements increase, but the reward is something original and distinctive, and, with luck, our projects may spark off your own ideas. Metallic stamping, for instance, is an area that has lots of potential: Fortuny-style velvets rich with gold or silver powder decoration, metal leaf motifs on furniture and walls. In each case, applying the design is straightforward, though the techniques may differ. The trickiest part is cutting your own stamp; unless you are very deft, it is wise to start with very simple motifs and go slowly. Rubber is so resilient that the knack of cutting more complicated shapes, such as our leaf design, comes with practice, and impatience could lead to cut fingers.

STAMPED
PLACE MATS

L ETTERS AND NUMBERS are fun and fashionable as motifs, but, failing a lucky find like ours, you could substitute any standard rubber stamps here. To be effective, the surface of your mats should be matt and absorbent, like blotting paper, to take the paint successfully.

YOU WILL NEED

A set of MDF 'blanks' in any shape or size
Acrylic primer
Matt emulsion (latex) paint
Standard brushes
Fine sandpaper
Stamps
Ink pads in various colours
Gloss acrylic varnish

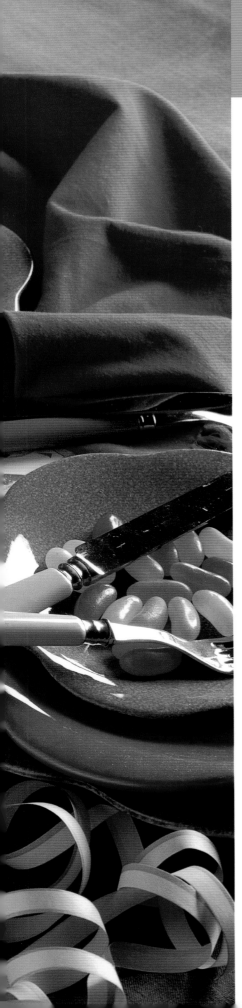

1 First, prepare the mats by smoothing the edges with sandpaper and base coating with acrylic primer. Sand smooth, then re-coat with matt emulsion (latex) paint.

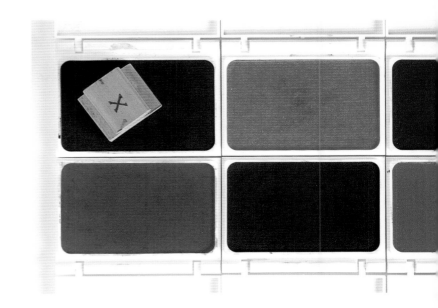

2 Stamp onto the mat, using letters or numbers in different colours scattered randomly over the surface. Letters would be decorative here, though you could make up words with them instead.

3 When complete, coat with two layers of gloss acrylic varnish to act as protection and to give the mats an attractive shine.

SILVEREDMIRROR FRAME

A RELIEF MOULDED PICTURE FRAME (the architectural term is 'bolection'), painted dark green, was stamped with size at intervals before applying silvery metal leaf. We used aluminium leaf, cheaper than silver and non-tarnishing, and conveniently available in little booklets of transfers.

YOU WILL NEED

Rotring rubber
Scalpel with extra blade
Wundasize (*see* p. 192)
Aluminium transfer leaf
Scissors
Soft, clean rag
Waxed paper plate
Acrylic varnish or PVA (optional)

1 A very simple design of two parallel stripes is cut from the rotring rubber. Draw the design on first, cut round the shapes in the same manner as a potato cut (*see* p. 40), then whittle away the background to leave the image 'proud' by several millimetres.

2 Dip the stamp in Wundasize. You may prefer to use standard Japan Gold size, which has varying drying times. Wundasize is more flexible, usable after 20 minutes, or up to 24 hours.

3 Stamp size stripes at regular intervals around the frame. The advantage of a hand-made stamp like this is that it bends round curves easily.

4 Use scissors to cut aluminium leaf sheets into smaller squares, just big enough to cover the 'stripes'.

5 Lay the cut squares, metal face down, over the stripes, pressing firmly on the back with fingertips. Carry on doing so round the frame.

63

6 Peel off the waxed backing from the metal squares. Don't expect it to come away leaving two perfect shapes: there will be loose bits and tags. But leave the frame for several hours to let the size harden before tidying these up.

7 Then, with a soft rag, wipe over the motifs to remove all the loose `skewings' and reveal neat repeat motifs. If any gaps in the leaf appear, re-size (use a brush) and re-leaf as before.

8 Rub the leaf gently but firmly with a clean rag to weld it still tighter to the surface and bring up the shine. Varnish, if liked, with acrylic varnish or PVA solution.

FORTUNY-STYLE
VELVET
TIE-BACK

T HIS IS JUST A TASTER to show what can be done in the way of glorifying pile fabric (or any other) with stamps, size and bronze powders. It is extraordinary how opulent ordinary cotton velveteen looks given this treatment. For further inspiration, read books about Fortuny (1871–1949), the Italian artist/designer whose velvet wraps, capes and coverlets in soft velvets decorated in gold and silver were greatly coveted when he started to design clothes from about 1906. Bronze powders (a generic name for a wide range of powders in all conceivable metallic shades) are essential for decorating fabrics because they are flexible and penetrate, whereas metal leaf would just sit on top and flake off.

YOU WILL NEED

Large rotring rubber
Scalpel
Pencil with eraser tip
Wundasize or PVA
Roller or brush
Old gold shade of bronze powder
Soft brush or cotton wool balls
Cheap face mask to guard against inhaling
   bronze powder

1 Draw out and cut
rubber stamp motif
in the same way
as a potato cut, as
described on p. 40.

2 Brush or roll Wundasize (PVA) over the stamp
and press firmly onto the fabric. Dab pencil eraser
into Wundasize and dot onto fabric. A slightly
more generous coat of size may be indicated
with pile fabrics, since it looks best if the design
strikes a little way into the pile. Repeat size
stamping at regular intervals, measured by eye.

3 Put on your mask, then tip metal powder into a clean glass jar with a wide mouth. With the soft brush or cotton wool balls, apply powder to the sized areas, extending over the edges slightly. *Or* spoon it carefully into a sprinkler, made by fitting a piece of net or gauze over a cardboard tube with a rubber band. Work powder well in with a brush.

4 When the fabric is completely stamped, hang it out of a window and shake well to remove the surplus powder. You will be charmed by the tidy way the motifs spring up and by the luxuriousness of the effect.

BATIK

BATIK IS THE MOST SOPHISTICATED and labour intensive of the various resist dyeing processes which have been used round the world through the many centuries since patterned cloth was preferred to plain. The technique, in which melted wax 'drawing' on fabric resists immersion in a dye-bath, is of uncertain origin, attributed by some to India, others to China. Yet it was in Ancient Egypt where a similar process was described by the Roman historian Pliny. Most likely, as with many good ideas and inventions, batik, or a variant, surfaced spontaneously in many parts of the world.

Where batik took root in its most sophisticated form, evolving into a textile art of breathtaking colour and complexity, and of near sacred significance, was Java, and especially the north coast of the island, historically a port of call on trade routes between East, West and points between. Merchants, missionaries, pirates, entrepreneurs, fortune hunters dropped anchor in northern ports like Surabaya, and the effect of these outside influences on a staid and inherently conservative society is fascinatingly recorded in the evolution of Javanese batik down the centuries, creating a multi-cultural mix of symbols and motifs which must be unique in textile history.

Religion, both Buddhism and Hinduism, imposed from outside, made its mark first on this traditional craft. The Javanese seem to have comfortably assimilated the two, to begin with,

Using a restricted but harmonious palette, this early central Javanese batik shows the filigree elaboration typical of the period and place.

seeing Buddha and Shiva as different aspects of the same divinity. Emblems of both religions – the lotus, or the interlocking circles of Hinduism – found their way into batik design, alongside indigenous motifs such as the *tumpal* – sets of equilateral triangles running the width of the cloth – and the tiny rice-grain dots, *isen,* which were used as background pattern.

By the thirteenth century, Hinduism seemed in control of the island, yet within a century, astonishingly, Java seems to have converted, very largely, to Islam. The reason for this was social as much as economic. Javanese merchants saw advantages in a faith which did away with the restrictive caste system and which encouraged trade with the Islamic countries, then the world's most powerful trading bloc. From this time forward, predictably, Islamic calligraphy and arabesques enter the batik repertoire, while representations of the human form, forbidden to Muslims, dwindle in importance.

In the meantime, increasingly remote cultural influences began to impinge on Javanese batik as foreign traders – notably Chinese and later Dutch – founded settlements on the island. Many of these intermarried with the Javanese, creating a new group within the society, known as *indische*, a somewhat ambiguous term comparable perhaps to 'creole' in the Americas. All of these added new elements to batik design, as batik workers incorporated Chinese dragons, lion-dogs and botanical motifs for the flower-mad Dutch.

An unusual batik from Eastern Europe, designed by Artur Lakatos and executed by Klara Roman in 1914.

The Dutch, around 1824, made a profound impression on batik by introducing a fine, machine-woven cotton known as *tjap sen*, which took the increasingly intricate designs better than the coarser native homespun. Many of the *indische* began designing and producing their own batiks, adding a whole new approach to the craft. Unlike the Javanese workers, predominantly women who seemed content with anonymity, this new breed of batik artists chose to personalize their work, executing their own designs from start to finish, which they distinguished with a small or flamboyant signature. These date largely from the late nineteenth century, and are notable for their use of 'fashionable' colours, often of Western derivation, for innovations such as plain backgrounds or flower designs with a naturalistic flow. It is debatable whether this influx of new ideas and fresh perspective revitalized an ancient technique or, as can happen when such an old-established and labour-intensive process is involved, hastened its decline by making it artistically self-aware and over-sophisticated.

Today, despite government encouragement, the production of high quality batik is fighting a losing battle against cheap, mass-produced imitations, a dwindling work force, and the high cost of imported cloth.

Batik, surprisingly, is not a word native to Java, though some scholars see a possible derivation from the Javanese word *titik*, meaning dot, or drop, which features in much traditional batik design, as a background 'filler' to the pattern.

From earliest times, batik work, hand executed, was done almost exclusively by women, unself-consciously perpetuating a tradition followed in spare moments in the home or in more organized workshops. Hand-drawn batik was called *tulis,* and it ruled for centuries until it was challenged in the nineteenth century by *cap,* a mass-production process using wooden or metal blocks to print the waxed designs. Because this required sustained effort and physical strength, *cap* batik became a largely male production.

In *tulis* work the only tool is a curious little copper bowl, attached to a wooden handle, with a small spout to one side through which the melted wax, encouraged by blowing up the spout, flows freely enough to draw the complex outlines characteristic of fine batik. This canting, or *djanting,* comes with many different-sized spouts, interchangeable according to whether bold outline or fine detail is required. The wax is kept liquid on a small earthenware charcoal stove, scooped up as needed by the canting. The cloth to be 'batiked' is suspended taut and flat over bamboo poles and before immersion into dye-baths is folded with great care. Because the resist is a wax with a low melting point, all dyeing processes must be cold or, at most, tepid, and a whole repertoire of special batik dyes was developed over time to give rich, lasting colours.

Each separately coloured element in a batik *tulis* design represents successive waxings, dyeings and subsequent clearing away of previous waxing – usually by scraping, followed by boiling. On the 'best' batik, the waxing is done on both sides of the cloth, making it reversible and doubling up this patient handiwork.

The basic principle of resist dyeing is easy enough to grasp, at least where the simpler two-colour prints of 'village batik' are concerned. For a white design on an indigo background, for example, all the design elements are waxed over, the cloth is then dipped into the indigo dye-bath until sufficient depth of colour is arrived at, then the waxed areas are scraped to reveal a white pattern on a blue background. However, the number of processes involved in producing a

Batik work in West Africa is entirely different in design from Javanese batik, as this display of handsome geometric cloth demonstrates.

quality batik in several colours is mind-boggling, and it would not be unusual for the completion of a sarong length of two metres to take over a year. First the cotton cloth must be boiled to remove any dressing, treated with oil and lye to make the fibres receptive to dyeing, boiled again, folded and beaten with mallets to soften the cloth to receive waxing. Next the design is drawn out in pencil, from memory and freehand in some cases, but more often via a tracing. The cloth is then ready for its first waxing. For a relatively simple, three-colour design of, say, red flowers and white detailing on an indigo ground, all the areas to remain white or red would be waxed to resist the first indigo dyeing. Next, to achieve the red

A gorgeous kaleidoscope of intricate coloured batik selected at random from a typical workshop in Thailand.

flowers, the wax is removed from the flowers, though not from the white detailing, and the entire blue ground is waxed over. The cloth is dipped in red dye this time, folded carefully to avoid cracking the wax and the whole cloth finally scraped free of wax to reveal red flowers, outlined and detailed in white, against a blue ground sprinkled with small background motifs. To set the dye, the batik is finally put into a bath of lime and water, before being stretched out on bamboo poles to dry and offered for sale.

This is still relatively straightforward compared to the processes involving many colours and over-dyeing. Traditional batik made use of four main colours derived from local plants, bark and roots. Blue came from indigo; a deep red, *mengkudu,* from bark and roots of *Morinda citrifolia*; yellow, *tegerang,* from the plant *Cudriana javanesis*; and a rich brown, *soga,* from the bark of a tree, *Pelthophorum ferrugineum.* Green was achieved by over-dyeing pale indigo with *tegerang* yellow, mauve by over-dyeing with red. Because batik dyes are used cold or lukewarm, a pharmacopoeia of secret ingredients and recipes has grown up to facilitate penetration of dyes into the batik and improve the finish of the cloth, and these include items as various as seeds, jaggery or palm sugar, bananas, even raw meat. With the introduction of aniline, naptha and, latterly, synthetic dyes, which are both easier to use and give quicker results, the colouring of batik cloth changed considerably, moving towards a new range of pastels, bright pinks, aqua, many shades of mauve. Despite the lavish flower-garden prettiness of some of the best examples, it is hard not to feel regret that showiness has triumphed over the simpler palette and robust colours produced by the earlier natural dyestuffs. Working within a limited colour range, drawing on a design vocabulary of real significance within their culture, the early Javanese batik workers produced masterpieces of textile art.

THE TECHNIQUE

TRADITIONAL BATIK WORKERS chiefly make use of a *djanting,* in many sizes, for precision work, outlining and filling in fine detail, though they resort to brushes for waxing large areas quickly. We have made use of both to illustrate the process. Though batik designs can be applied readily with other means, as shown in our projects, mastering the use of the *djanting* is the first step to real freedom in the creation and application of batik patterns. Start with two *djantings,* in sizes corresponding to thick and thin pencil lines, and practise with them on a piece of fabric before embarking on a serious project. Don't fill the *djanting* too full when scooping up melted wax, or you may get splashes. A little kitchen paper wrapped round the bowl will help prevent drips, though these 'mistakes' can be decorative in themselves in the right context.

Experts recommend Japanese brushes for batik, because they are bushy enough to hold plenty of wax but still taper to a fine point in use. They should be cleaned in white spirit (mineral spirits) after use. To maintain wax at a constant temperature, many batik artists use a specially designed wax pot, available from craft shops. This operates like a slow cooker, keeping the wax melted without overheating. A *bain-marie* arrangement, with the wax container sitting in a just simmering pan of water, can be substituted. On no account melt wax over direct heat.

Now the wax. Indonesian batik workers have their own secret recipes, adding plant resins and suchlike to the wax for specific purposes. We used a 50/50 mixture of beeswax and paraffin-wax, obtainable in pellets, to give a wax which is neither too runny nor too sticky.

Lastly, the dyes. These must be coldwater, or at most tepid (like indigo), dyes for the obvious reason that boiling or even hot water would dissolve the waxed designs. Any coldwater dyes can be used, though professionals recommend Procion for their wide range of vivid colours, which are intermixable.

YOU WILL NEED

Pencil and ruler and/or set square
Two *djantings*
Japanese bristle brushes
Wax pot or *bain-marie*
Beeswax/paraffin-wax pellets
Coldwater dyes
Newspaper or kitchen roll

A WOODEN FRAME for stretching out the fabric is not essential, and in Indonesia is rarely used, but it is helpful while you are learning the craft as it keeps the fabric taut but springy and gives maximum control.

1 A basic batik kit is assembled, with brush and *djantings,* here shown resting on the wax pot.

2 Fabric stretched over a wooden frame is secured by coloured pins.

3 For a simple, regular design of circles, the fabric is first marked up with pencil and set square into squares to receive the pattern. The pencil marks will later be hidden by the dye.

4 Equal quantities of the two waxes are melted in the wax pot till liquefied, stirring to mix well.

6 The brush is dipped into the melted wax and used in the conventional way, re-dipping when the wax runs out. After use it should be cleaned in a jar of white spirit (mineral spirits), but don't leave it standing in the solvent or the bristles will bend out of shape.

5 The *djanting* is used to scoop some wax from the pot, and then employed to trace out a design on the fabric. It is held at an angle to the work, and moved steadily and fluently over the design, taking care not to spill wax. This comes easier with practice.

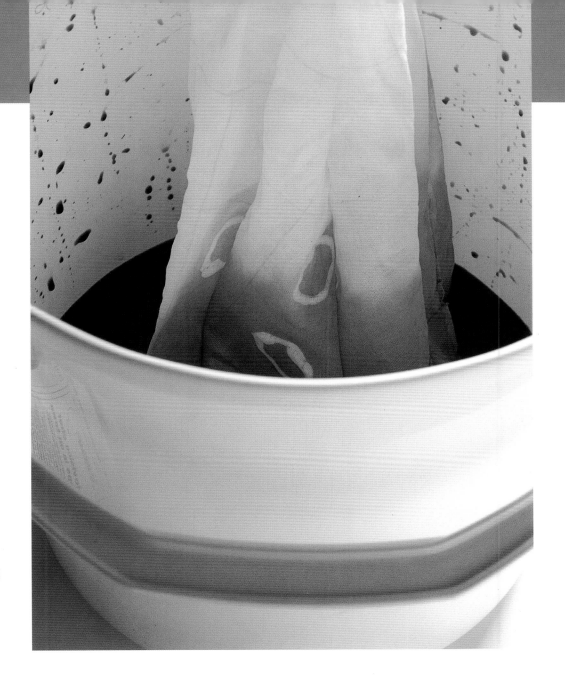

7 Once the waxing is done, the cloth is dipped in dye, fished out and hung up to dry.

8 The wax is then melted off by ironing it between sheets of newsprint or kitchen roll (*see* p. 83).

INDONESIAN BATIK ARTISTS go to pains to avoid cracking the wax designs while dyeing, disliking the adventitious 'craquelure' effect this gives. Lengths of cloth are carefully folded to fit into shallow but wide dye-baths. If, on the contrary, you like the crackled effect – and it is one which can be made into a positive feature – the fabric can be crushed up to fit a smaller receptacle. Batik on silk for clothing is usually sent to be dry-cleaned after the wax has been largely taken off by ironing, to remove the last slight stiffness remaining.

RUST-COLOURED
THROW

T HE WAX FOR THIS PROJECT was applied with a wire stamp, home-made from a fairly heavy gauge wire, and two stamps were used, one for the main body of the throw and a second for the border. This technique might raise eyebrows among traditionalists, but it opens up interesting possibilities for 'contemporary' batik.

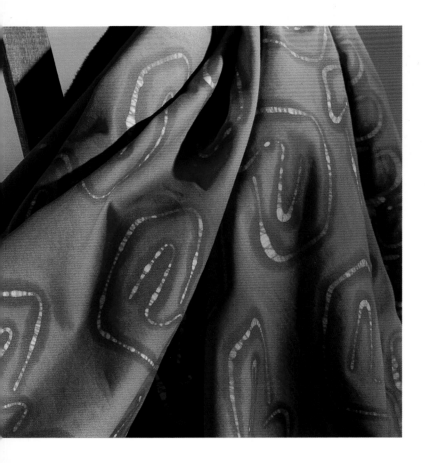

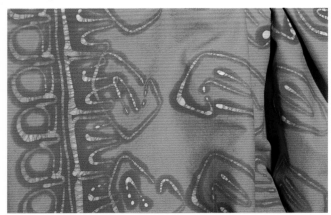

YOU WILL NEED

Sturdy wire
Pliers
Length of fabric, previously washed (we used
    lightweight calico)
Beeswax/paraffin-wax pellets
Procion (*see* p. 191) coldwater dye
Frame for stretching fabric (optional)

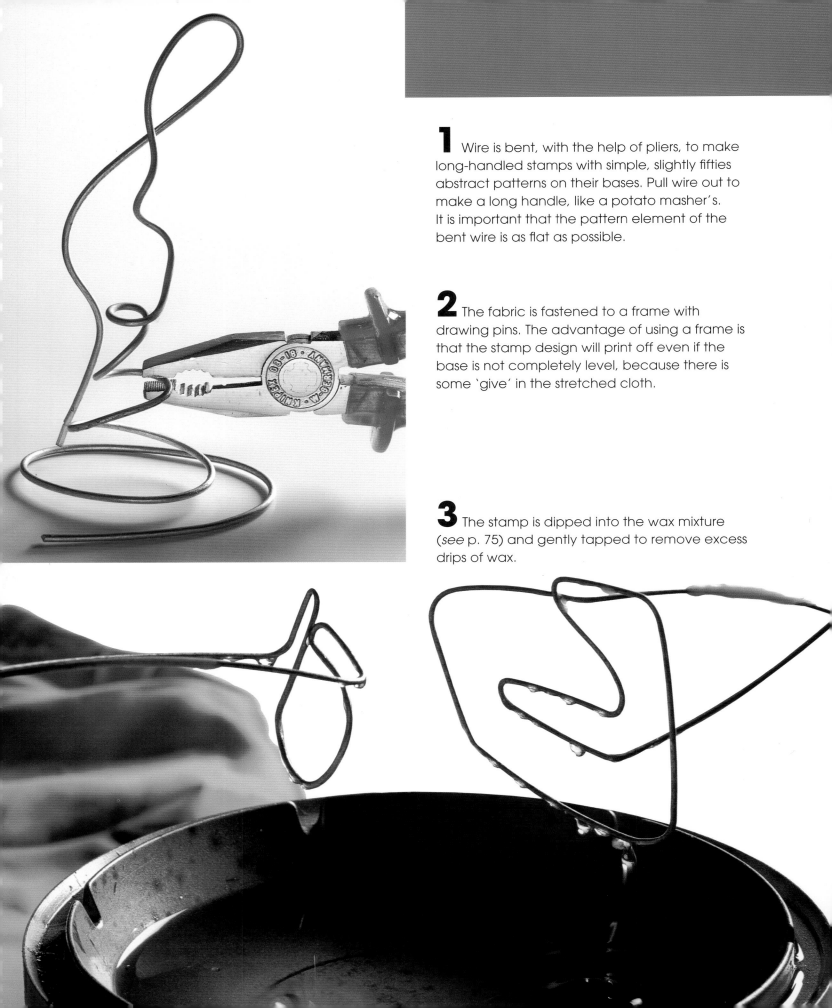

1 Wire is bent, with the help of pliers, to make long-handled stamps with simple, slightly fifties abstract patterns on their bases. Pull wire out to make a long handle, like a potato masher's. It is important that the pattern element of the bent wire is as flat as possible.

2 The fabric is fastened to a frame with drawing pins. The advantage of using a frame is that the stamp design will print off even if the base is not completely level, because there is some 'give' in the stretched cloth.

3 The stamp is dipped into the wax mixture (*see* p. 75) and gently tapped to remove excess drips of wax.

4 The stamp is pressed firmly down onto the fabric. The border stamp was applied in a tight continuous pattern, while the centre is stamped at fairly regular intervals, varying the direction of the motif.

5 The waxed fabric, unfastened from the frame, is dipped in Procion coldwater dye and dried flat.

6 The dry fabric is ironed between layers of newsprint to remove wax, which can be seen here seeping through the paper. This ironing may have to be repeated several times to clear the wax completely, although for some purposes a little wax left provides useful stiffening and a faint sheen.

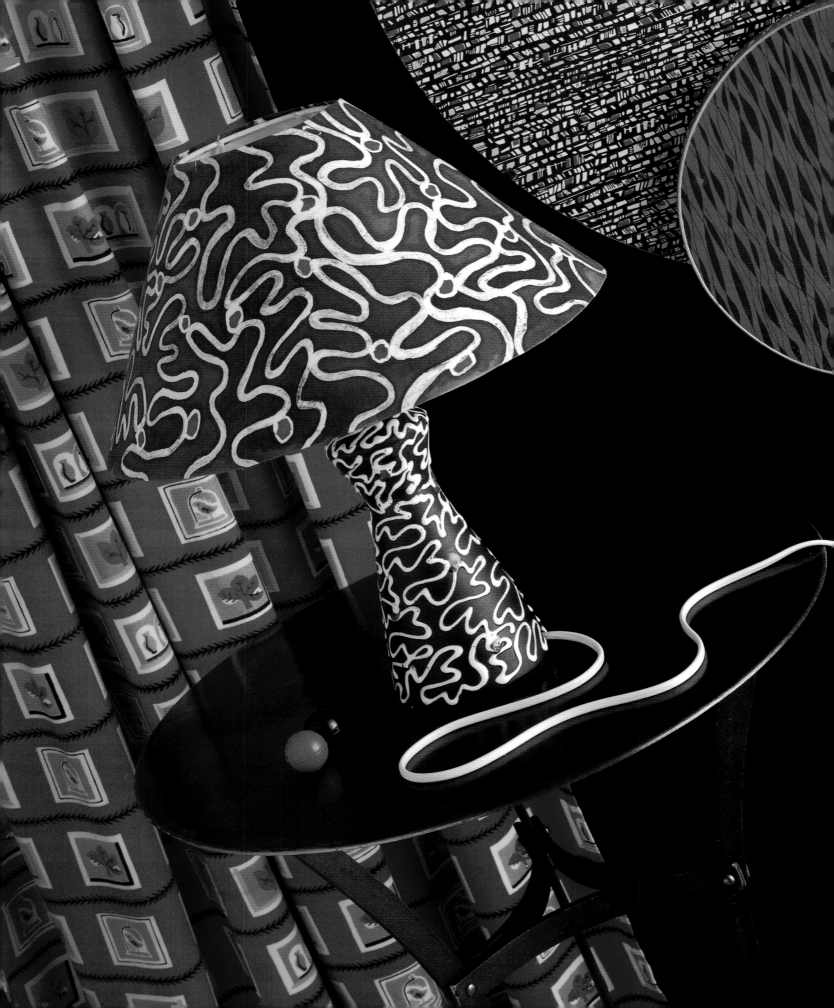

BATIK LAMPSHADE

T HE DESIGN FOR THIS BATIK LAMPSHADE has a trendy fifties feel to complement the genuine fifties lamp base. It also conveniently lends itself to brush application of the dyes used, since the waxed motif entirely enclosed the red blob, which was painted directly onto the fabric. The black background colour was likewise brushed on. Brushing paints directly onto fabric is always worth considering when you are planning a batik design, since it cuts out a second waxing (over the red blob here) and dyeing, and speeds the process up. However, it is best reserved for small projects and ones where colour fastness (as here) is not critical. Over a large piece of fabric it would undoubtedly be quicker to wax over the red motifs, and then dip the fabric into a black dye.

YOU WILL NEED

Strong cotton fabric
Frame for stretching fabric
Beeswax/paraffin-wax pellets
Fine watercolour brush and a larger Japanese
   brush
Deka fabric paints (*see* p. 191) in red and black
Self-adhesive lampshade backing (from craft
   shops)
Wire lampshade frame
Clear impact adhesive
Scissors
Pencil

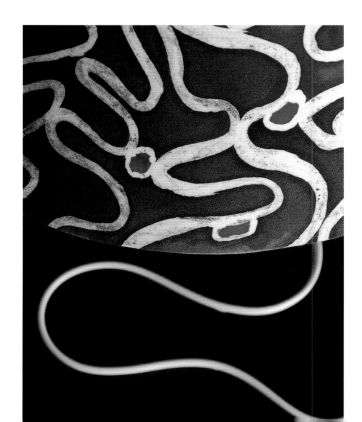

1 Trace out the outline of the lampshade onto the fabric, using an existing shade as a template. This can be done without dismantling the shade, using a sheet of newspaper or brown paper trimmed to fit over it exactly.

2 Stretch and pin the fabric over the stretching frame; lightly pencil on motifs for waxing.

3 Using the large Japanese brush dipped in wax, outline the motifs, keeping within the pencil lines, which will be covered by the fabric paint colours.

4 Paint red fabric paint directly onto fabric with the watercolour brush, covering the pencil lines of these 'spot' motifs.

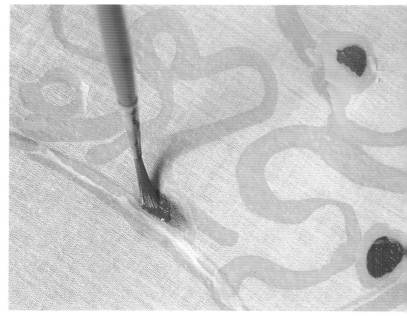

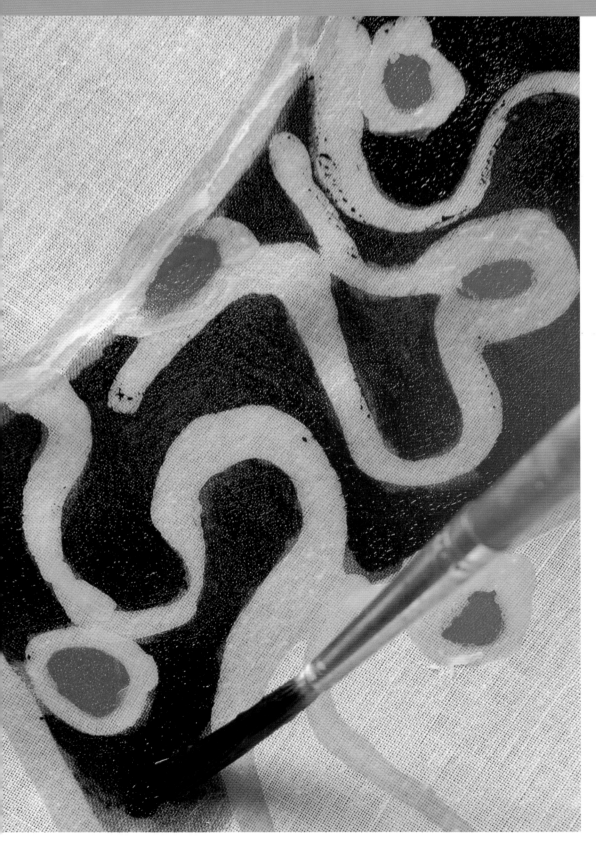

5 With the larger brush and black fabric paint, fill in the background of the design in black.

6 Unpin the fabric, iron off the wax, and cut out the shade along the pencilled outline.

7 Cut lampshade backing using the painted piece as a pattern, but trimming approximately a quarter of an inch or just under a centimetre off top and bottom.

8 Peel backing off the lampshade lining and attach to the wrong side of the batik, smoothing out carefully. Use a clear impact adhesive to join the two ends of the shade around the metal frame, over-lapping to make a neat seam. With the same adhesive, fold over the extra fabric along top and bottom of the frame and glue down. The bottom edge will need to be nicked all round to make it stretch to fit.

TIEDYE

TIE DYEING IS ANOTHER VERSION of the resist approach to making patterns on cloth, with the difference that areas of the fabric are tied, stitched, folded and otherwise manipulated to prevent the dye reaching them, thus making patterns which can be large or small, loose or precise, depending on the methods used to prepare the fabric beforehand. Tie dyeing is the most accessible of the techniques for patterning fabrics described in this book, partly because so little equipment is needed – rubber bands, string, a packet of dye is enough to create simple but spectacular effects – and partly, no doubt, because the immense popularity of DIY tie dye in the sixties and seventies has familiarized a whole generation with its engaging simplicity and the wide range of patterns that can be produced without special skills and with minimum outlay. However, the downside of this is that anything too easy rapidly becomes banal in a world spoilt for novelty. One T-shirt with a tie-dyed bull's-eye motif is fun, thousands are a yawn.

Our aim in this section is to re-instate tie dye as a valid process for patterning fabric, combining the complex (folding) or the laborious (stitching) with the easy-peasy – paper clips, rubber bands, etc. – to create patterns of a complexity that does not immediately read as 'oh yes, tie and dye again'.

Historically, this is closer to the use of tie and dye techniques in countries like India, where labour was cheap and resources limited. Learned treatises on tie dye are conspicuous by their absence, but it seems safe to say that techniques

Cloth drying after it has been dyed, with the ties still in place, in the traditional hand-manufactured 'Gara' tie dye of Sierra Leone.

like those shown here have been used for centuries in rural areas to glorify cheap local textiles, for domestic use, and also for commercial purposes. The patience and repetitive tedium of tying rice grains or tiny pebbles individually into a cheap calico would deter most Westerners, but it is noticeable from a glance round any retail outlet featuring ethnic artefacts how many of these still rely on these mind-bogglingly painstaking processes for much of their effect. Recent, single colour prints often exhibit a combination of techniques, batik for complex patterns, offset by a background of sprinkled dots or circles that suggest tie dye techniques.

With practice and patience, tie dye patterns, as seen on Indian tablecloths and bedcovers, can become standardized and largely predictable, or ninety-five per cent predictable, allowing for a small margin of human error. But to the Western mind, a great deal of the excitement and fun and appeal of tie dyeing resides precisely in the unpredictibility of the outcome. Chance enters into the finished product rather as it does in the final appearance of glazed ceramics after firing, an element of happenstance which is part of the reward. With more sophisticated processes, such as batik, what you see is what you get, but even professional craftspeople admit that unwrapping, unfolding and untying a piece of tie-dyed cloth carries a little thrill of anticipation because no two pieces are ever exactly alike. However, as they point out, for the best, sharpest results some patience is needed, because the items should be left to dry out naturally.

Choice of fabric can make a big difference to the look of a tie-dyed item. Natural fibres, such as silk, cotton, linen or wool, dye most successfully and give the clearest patterning. Finely woven cloth, like cotton lawn or fine soft silk, is especially rewarding, giving a subtle variety of colour tones, and a look of glamour and luxury to the finished item.

A detail of brilliantly tinted liquid from Bali, Indonesia.

THE TECHNIQUE

THE TWO PROCESSES DETAILED BELOW were chosen to illustrate the variety of patterns obtainable with tie dye techniques. The first, laughably simple, bundles chickpeas individually into cotton fabric, securing them with rubber bands. Dyed, this leaves natty little white rings. The second process is more intricate, involving folding, rolling and tying cotton lawn at regular intervals, to produce a complex and impressive chevron design. It comes as no surprise to learn that this is a traditional Indian tie dye process, originally developed to make patterned lengths of cloth for turbans. The result is a real tribute to the ingenuity of rural craftspeople, and a triumph of skill over limited means.

TIEDYED **CIRCLES**

YOU WILL NEED

Length of cloth – calico, lawn, etc.
Packet of chickpeas and/or haricot beans,
    red-eyed beans, etc.
Rubber bands
Pencil
Coldwater dye (we used Procion)

1 The fabric length was marked with pencil dots beforehand to keep spacing regular – harder to do by eye once the tying has begun because the fabric gets scrunched up. Here we see the process under way, with beans and peas tightly secured into the cloth with rubber bands.

2 The fabric has been dipped into a vivid green dye made up following maker's instructions. Wet colour tends to dry lighter, but it gives a fair indication of what to expect. If the colour seems wishy-washy, re-dip till it is as you want.

3 After drying out naturally (which may take hours, or days) the unwrapping begins, revealing a simple but charming design.

4 Once ironed, the full appeal of the cloth can be appreciated.

CHEVRON

YOU WILL NEED

Length of fine white cotton lawn, previously
    washed
Strong waxed twine
Coldwater dye (we used a rich purple)

1 The cloth is folded concertina-wise in pleats about 3 inches (8cm) wide.

2 The strip is then rolled at a 45 degree angle, along its length, and bound with twine as tightly as possible at regularly spaced intervals.

3 The tied piece is dipped in its purple dye-bath and then retrieved. Wooden tongs are useful tools for lifting cloth in and out. They prevent you staining your hands, or in the case of hot water dyes, scalding your fingers.

4 Use sharp scissors to cut the ties once the fabric has dried out naturally, taking care not to cut the fabric.

5 The chevron pattern emerged crinkled, and was then smoothed out by ironing, which is when the full complexity of colour and pattern can be appreciated.

PAPERCLIPS

F ERROUS SULPHATE IS A NATURAL rust dye which emerges from the dye-bath greenish yellow, gradually changing to a glorious tawny orange. A caustic soda or washing soda solution is needed to fix the dye and make it permanent. Caustic soda works more rapidly but needs caution in handling. Washing soda is innocuous but slower to take effect. For details see p. 192.

YOU WILL NEED

Length of fabric (we used heavy-textured silk)
Box of standard size paper clips
Ferrous sulphate
Caustic soda or washing soda solution

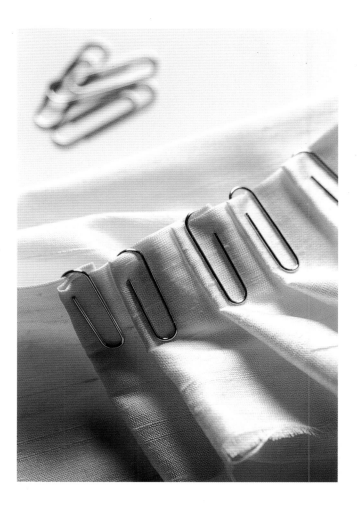

1 The silk was first folded concertina-wise, then small tucks were made across the folds and secured with paper clips top and bottom, letting the centre part open out as shown.

2 This process is carried out along the whole length of the fabric, and it is well worth taking the time to secure neat folds.

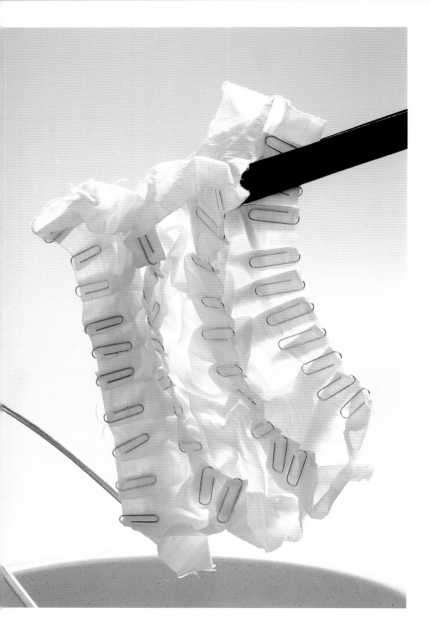

3 The fabric length is dunked in the dye-bath and into the caustic or washing soda dip, and at this point is coloured a drab olive. If the colour is not intense enough, the fabric can be dipped again into the dye solution, then the fixative, repeating till the colour intensity looks right. The colour change from green to rusty orange begins within minutes but is not fully developed till the fabric has dried.

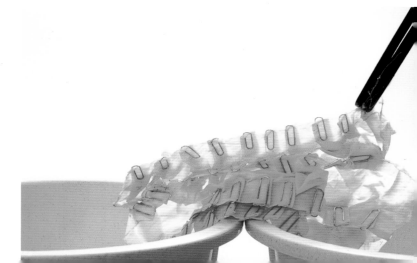

4 Remove the paper clips from the tawny golden dyed silk once it is thoroughly dry.

5 We decided to use the silk to cover heavy-duty card to make a particularly luxurious document folder. Here the well-ironed silk is being measured up with ruler and scalpel.

INDIGOCUSHIONS

T HIS IS A PROJECT WITH DIRECT LINKS to traditional Indian tie dye practice, both in the use of indigo and in the simple, if painstaking, means of creating a pattern. Painstaking? This will depend on how fast you sew, making long tacking (basting) stitches. Many people would find this quicker than tying grains of rice individually. The result is charming, fine herringbone stripes against a dappled indigo blue. Indigo dye is intriguing to use, because of its dramatic colour change, and it remains deservedly the most popular of all the natural dyestuffs. It is made from the leaves of the indigo plant, native to Africa, South-East Asia and South America. It is a substantive dye, requiring no mordant to fix it. However, natural indigo does need preparing to a formula, using a solution of washing soda and colour-run remover, to make it permanent. The formula and preparation of the dye are given in a separate section on p. 105.

YOU WILL NEED

Length of cotton lawn, or similar finely woven
  fabric
Large darning needle and stout thread
Indigo dye solution cooled to 30°C for cotton,
  50°C for silk/wool (*see* p. 105)

1 The pattern starts once more with concertina folds, regularly spaced. Then, with a needle and length of thread longer than the cloth, begin oversewing the folds as shown using evenly spaced stitches and carrying on to the end, but leaving the spare thread hanging.

2 The folds, stitched above and below along their whole length, are then tightly gathered up by pulling up the loose threads to give the result shown here. The need for a fine, soft fabric becomes clear – gathering up a heavier weight fabric would probably snap the thread.

3 The prepared fabric is dipped into the cooled dye-bath and left for between five to fifteen minutes, submerged. Remove carefully and hang up to dry. At this stage it will be a drab olive shade.

4 As air gets to the cloth it will gradually turn blue. If the blue is not intense, repeat the dyeing process. When the colour is satisfactory, the fabric should be left to dry naturally, which may take several days.

5 The threads can either be unpicked or withdrawn by pulling gently at one end.

6 Ironing shows up the tie-dyed motif in all its charm and finesse. We made it up into a cushion cover, but I can visualize it on lawn or silk making an enviable shirt to wear with blue jeans, with a long matching scarf, perhaps.

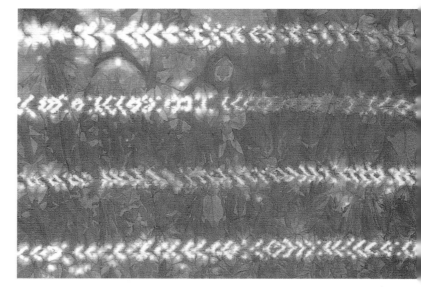

INDIGO

INDIGO IS OBTAINABLE both as a natural and a synthetic dye. The synthetic version is chemically the same, but stronger, so half as much is needed. We used the natural indigo because we wanted the real thing, an inimitable radiant blue, of great permanence. Making up the dye-bath sounds complicated, first time round, but experts maintain that with care and practice indigo is one of the easiest and most satisfactory dyes to use.

Preparing the dye-bath, and using it, can be messy – drips will stain permanently – so is best done outside, with plastic sheet to catch the drips and rubber gloves to protect hands. Anyone with respiratory problems should wear a mask while working with colour-run remover.

YOU WILL NEED

Natural indigo dye in powder form
Colour-run remover (Beckmann's or RIT –
   see p. 191)
Washing soda
Jam-making thermometer
Heat-proof glass jar
Stainless steel dye-pan
The quantities given will make up 1 gallon
   (4 litres) of dye.

DISSOLVE 2oz (50g) washing soda in 1 table-spoon boiling water in an old glass jar and let cool. Mix two teaspoons natural indigo into a paste with two tablespoons warm water, then gradually add the washing soda solution, stirring until the indigo is fully dissolved and no gritty bits remain. Pour 1 gallon (4 litres) water into steel dye-pan and heat to 50°C. Add indigo solution to pan and gently mix together. Now sprinkle 1oz (25g) colour-run remover on the surface, and leave for 30–60 minutes at a constant temperature. By now the liquid should have turned from blue to yellow-green. If the liquid is still blue, add a little more colour-run remover and wait again. If a blue film remains on the surface, due to oxygenation, this can be blotted up with kitchen paper before dyeing the cloth. For cotton or linen the liquid should be cooled to 30°C, but wool or silk can go in immediately. All fabrics should be thoroughly wetted before dyeing but well-squeezed to remove excess water before immersion.

LINO CUTTING
AND PRINTING

W HILE NOT SO DURABLE as wood blocks, lino cuts are considerably easier to produce, requiring no special skills or expensive equipment. Lino blocks are available in a wide range of pre-cut sizes, and a beginner will be able to cut interesting designs with as few as two or three carving tools, or cutters: 'V'-shaped for finer linear cuts, and 'U'-shaped gouges for cutting away the background to leave the design or image in relief. Lino has a consistency not unlike hard cheese, offering some resistance but yielding readily to sharp tools and steady pressure, making it a satisfying material to sculpt.

As usual, the nature of the material dictates to a large extent the style of execution. Lino cuts lend themselves to strong, somewhat stylized images, their bold expressiveness compensating for the lack of fine detail obtainable with woodcuts. Their graphic quality makes them well suited to fabric printing, among other things. Edward Bawden (1903–89), who designed wallpaper and fabrics as well as being a notable British artist of the inter-war period, quite often worked with lino cuts and clearly enjoyed exploring the bold simplification imposed by his material. Even if your bent is towards the purely decorative, it is always rewarding to study an artist's work in the medium. Bawden lived in Essex for most of his working life, and a tiny

ABOVE *A lino-cut by the master Edward Bawden (1903-89) designed as a book illustration for 'The Ant and the Grasshopper', one of Aesop's Fables.*

OPPOSITE *A selection of hand-blocked wallpapers by Katherine Morris, who works both with antique motifs, such as the floral prints here, and new lino cuts, like the 'reversible' sun motifs.*

Examples of contemporary hand lino-blocked fabrics by Susan Bosence, who works frequently with small repeat motifs and organic dyes.

museum in Saffron Walden, the Fry Gallery, holds a collection of his later work, which is well worth a visit. Bawden's star, like that of his friend and contemporary, Eric Ravilious (1903–42), is definitely on the ascendant, as a quintessentially British painter of his period, with a style that is intensely personal and immediately recognizable.

If you are comparing lino cuts with stencils as a means of printing your own designs, on fabric, paper or what have you, there seems to be little to differentiate the results, aesthetically. A stencilled length of fabric or paper will not look very different from a lino cut print of the same design, though the need for 'bridges' on a stencil (*see* p. 192) will give the game away if you know what you are looking for. From the executant's point of view, however, the lino cut motif scores in that it can be repeated, once cut, with much less effort than a hand-brushed stencil. A quick pass with a roller, and a sharp tap with a mallet, or rolling pin, and the print is there – sharp, complete and endlessly repeatable. Rapid effectiveness is of the essence of printing. The creative work goes into the 'master' – block, lino cut, potato cut – and after that the rest is plain sailing. In a subtle way, this makes the artist, decorator or printer the master of his or her process, even somewhat detached from it, in a way in which a stenciller, endlessly repeating a series of physical actions of quite a complex sort, can never aspire to. This is not a value judgement. Those with a creative drive and curiosity to match will try most of these processes as a matter of course, and with luck fasten upon the one most suited to their talent and temperament.

LINO BLOCK WALLPAPER

LINO CUTS CAN BE USED to print exceptionally handsome hand-blocked wallpaper. The process is no slower than hand-blocking fabric, the materials are cheap, and the results impressive enough to have attracted a number of artists, working for themselves or on commission. An early exponent of the technique was a remarkable American woman, Esther Stevens Brazer, a collateral descendent of the celebrated eighteenth-century patriot and designer Paul Revere, and something of a mover and shaker in her own right. 'Research and preservation of early American decoration,' one of her daughters recalls, 'was the most important thing in mother's life.' Esther Brazer was passionate about historic houses. If she found a fine specimen in the wrong place, she simply had the entire edifice transported bodily and reconstructed in her chosen location. 'She was never idle. Her hands were always busy,' her daughter adds, noting that she would while away the time at the orthodontist's by cutting stencils 'while we waited'.

While she was restoring the Hicks House in Cambridge, Massachusetts, Esther Brazer noticed that 'great wads of wallpaper stripped from the walls of an upstairs bedroom were lying about the floor . . . these thick scraps floated in the bathtub and lo and behold! out of this "waste" I found remnants of fifteen layers of wallpaper. Most researchers would have stopped there but I went on to the hand reproduction of the three oldest designs because they so ideally suited the simple forthrightness of the house.' Two she reproduced via stencils, but a block-printed pattern she decided to recreate with a lino cut. According to her daughter, she then 'printed it by placing the paper and inked block on the floor and standing

Lino-cut blocks from Susan Bosence's fabric printing studio, together with dye-pot and pad.

An extraordinarily attractive lino-cut wallpaper, 'Sahara', designed by Edward Bawden in 1928, is a witty example of Art Deco stylization.

on it to produce sufficient pressure for the print . When Mrs Brazer moved to her next period home, an old tavern which was 'flaked' – that is, disassembled and reconstructed, timber by timber, fifty miles away – she naturally felt reluctant to abandon her hand-blocked paper, and instead steamed it off carefully and had it rehung in her second home, re-christened Grays Garden House. A smudgy black-and-white photograph of the thirties shows a demure pattern of floral motifs arranged in stripes, in a light colour on a medium-toned ground, admirably setting off Mrs Brazer's collection of antiques and a splendid portrait of George Washington.

Here, it seems to me, is an idea worth bearing in mind if you have a house to restore in period and are lucky enough to turn up an exceptionally pretty wallpaper while making good. Even if you were able to track down a modern facsimile – and 'document papers' are eagerly collected today – it would be unlikely to survive in its original colouring. Manufacturers, reprehensibly in my view, regularly reissue old designs with new, updated colourings, thereby frequently – as is the case with some of the Morris papers – coarsening or enfeebling the original.

If cutting your own lino block and printing several rolls of paper is a pipe dream, there are designers who will do this for you. It might seem retrograde in the late twentieth century to set up shop as a purveyor of hand-blocked papers, operating as a one-man or more usually one-woman band, but the materials are cheap, the results are decidedly handsome, and the process has always attracted artists/craftspersons.

The late Peggy Angus, known as the Grand Old Lady of Lino Cutting, became famous in a small way for her lino-blocked wallpaper designs. As a young woman she was a close friend of Edward Bawden, who often stayed with his friend Eric Ravilious in her primitive but magnificently situated cottage on the Sussex Downs; they did some of their best work there in the 1930s. Bawden's vigorous use of lino cuts must have influenced Peggy Angus, who developed the idea of lino-blocked wallpapers, in two colours, using her own designs.

Katherine Morris, who operates from a studio flat in Covent Garden, London, worked with Peggy Angus as a student, helping her with the repetitive work of printing lino cuts over rolls of lining paper.

Though trained as an architect, she finds more satisfaction creating and printing her own lino cut designs on commission. She readily concedes the influence of Peggy Angus, both artistically and technically. Like Peggy, she restricts herself to two colours. 'Peggy thought wallpapers should be backgrounds, something that wouldn't compete with paintings and pictures. They could be richly coloured, but subdued, like damask. She didn't really approve of the hand-blocked designs, like Morris's, using several colours. She felt they were too competitive.'

Katherine cuts lino, 5 mm (¼ in) thick, into designs 28 cm (11 in) square, using three or four lino cutting tools of varying shapes and sizes. Like Peggy, she prints onto 30 metre lengths of lining paper, previously coated with a standard emulsion paint. She uses a particular range of trade emulsions, in historic colours, for all her work. Emulsion (latex) paints, fast-drying, reasonably permanent (she applies an invisible glaze for special situations, bathrooms, kitchens, etc.) are ideal for her work, she explains. The colour range is very wide, and includes what professionals call 'good colours', strong, saturated blues, reds, yellows, as well as a choice of the low-voltage neutrals the eighteenth century specified for hallways, stairs, the public areas of domestic housing, and described as 'common colours', 'stone colours' or, more succinctly, 'drab'.

'Drabness' was not a pejorative term then, and looking at some of Katherine's low-key papers, one can see why – restrained, but quietly effective, these would make a telling background in a period house or, indeed, a contemporary studio flat. But as Katherine insists, the beauty of her hand-blocked process is its flexibility (see her designs on p. 106). The same design, printed up in different colourways, changes character dramatically, muted in some cases, explosively colourful in others. She is often asked to match a paper to a fabric, or furnishings already in place, and this is no problem. Her dream is to execute a one-off design expressing a client's chosen theme in their preferred colours for a particular room. The idea seems luxuriously self-indulgent, perhaps, but the cost, compared with commercial hand-blocked papers, is surprisingly modest. Like Peggy Angus, her mentor, Katherine is an enthusiast, pursuing a patient craft with care and dedication, buoyed up through all the repetitious slog of colouring the block, registering the block, applying the right amount of pressure on the block, by the artist's passionate curiosity to see what emerges, how it compares with earlier versions, whether it is a triumph or a disappointment. This seeking, at once passionate and coolly objective, is at the root of most of the byways and offshoots of the printing process and its many variants described in this book.

THE TECHNIQUE

WE SETTLED ON a simple, spirally motif to demonstrate the use of different lino gouges, 'V'-shaped for incising clean lines and the 'U'-shaped gouge for clearing away the background to leave the motif in relief. Always warm the lino – by putting it onto a radiator, for example – before cutting the pattern: warm lino will pare away like cheese, whereas cold lino may chip and snap.

YOU WILL NEED

A lino block 4–5 inches (about 12 cm) square
An off-cut of chipboard, cut to the same size
Carbon paper and pencil
Impact or woodworking adhesive
'V'-shaped and 'U'-shaped lino gouges
Small roller
Printing ink

Sticking the lino to a chipboard block with double-sided tape first makes cutting easier as it gives you something chunky to get hold of. Some people make a small wooden frame, with two fixed right-angled sides, to keep the block steady and give something to push against while cutting.

1 The design is traced off with a sharp pencil onto the lino through a sheet of carbon paper.

2 Use a pencil to firm up the transferred design. With the 'V'-shaped gouge, cut round the inner spirals, then the outline of the motif with its four 'curls'.

3 Switching to the 'U'-shaped gouge, start paring away the surrounding lino in orderly parallel lines, as shown. Cut away from the motif to avoid cutting into it by mistake.

4 Printing should be done on a level surface. It is a good idea to pad the printing table slightly, with sheets of newspaper or an old blanket, when printing fabric. Whatever material is being printed should be stretched taut and fastened down with drawing pins or staples.

5 Lino printing ink is rolled onto the block using a small rubber roller, before reversing the design onto the chosen surface and using hand pressure, a tap with a mallet, a roll with a rolling pin or whatever method you choose for printing off the design. A little experimentation will show you how much pressure is needed.

MORRIS PRINT
TABLECLOTH

THE PRETTY, FRONDY DESIGN used for our lino-blocked tablecloth is not a copy, more 'in the style of' the revered and remarkable nineteenth-century designer, poet, weaver socialist and altogether lovable – as well as exceptionally gifted – figure of his time. Most of William Morris's designs used several colours, but we settled for a straightforward single colour print, shown here in green on the block, but printed off for the tablecloth in a delicious heathery mauve.

Lino blocks are, of course, as effective for fabric printing as they are for paper. We used a cheap calico (even cheaper by the bolt from a wholesaler), washed, dried and ironed beforehand. This is essential with calico, which usually comes with a degree of 'dressing' and also shrinks unpredictably on washing. Washing improves the texture of calico, anyway, leaving it softer and progressively whiter. Use a fabric paint for printing, because any tablecloth will need frequent washing. Alternatively, there are fabric mediums available, which are added to emulsion (latex) or acrylic paints to give them the necessary bonding qalities without stiffness.

If the calico is not wide enough for your purposes, the cloth will need to be seamed. But don't simply stitch two lengths together, leaving an unattractive seam down the middle of the cloth and hence your table. Cut one length in two and stitch one of these pieces, selvedge to selvedge, to each side of your main piece. This is best done before printing so that you can then keep the blocked design flowing continuously over the cloth. Hemming can be done before or after printing. Iron machine seams open and flat with a damp cloth.

Provide yourself with a 'print table' (*see* p. 191) to make the printing go smoothly and give clean, sharp results. This is an overall design, making accurate registration of the block more important. Professionals would probably go to some trouble to ensure this, laying threads across the table and fabric, secured at both ends. But a lot of people muddle through, gauging by eye, with good results.

By comparison with our other lino cut designs, this is unusually delicate in effect. Cutting the block for a graceful, linear motif like this is more demanding, but remember to warm the lino before cutting, go patiently, and you will be pleased with the outcome. As you can see, the lino cut itself is a beautiful object, worthy of framing. This is craftsmanship. Your first attempt may not look so elegant, but you will still feel proud of the resulting print.

YOU WILL NEED

Lino, and a piece of chipboard for backing
Lino cutting gouges
Pencil
Ruler or measuring tape
Masking tape
Oil-based fabric printing inks
Roller
Piece of glass, thick and bevelled
Palette knife
Lengths of calico
Printing table
Drawing pins or staple gun

1 Cut your lino block, as described on p. 112, gluing the design to a piece of chipboard cut to fit. Leave under pressure until dry.

2 Stretch the calico taut over the print table, using drawing pins or staples to hold it in place. Either start in the middle and work outwards, or start from one side and work across.

3 Place two strips of masking tape, at right angles, to mark the vertical and horizontal confines of the printing – a great help when registering the block.

4 Mark the centre of where the block will fall with pencil. For an overall print, a full block print will alternate with what is called a 'half block' repeat along the edge of your printed cloth. The pencil mark allows you to position this accurately.

5 Blue and yellow printing inks are mixed together with a palette knife on a piece of thick glass. The glass should have bevelled – not sharp – edges, so that it is safe to handle.

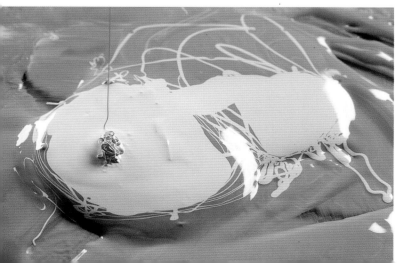

6 To achieve a good shade of grey-green, we dribbled white printing ink into the mixture.

7 Roll the mixed paint over your block and print a 'test' on a spare piece of cloth. Then position the block carefully onto your prepared cloth and print, using hand pressure, or a mallet or rolling-pin. Try all of these methods as you go along. Variations in definition will not spoil, indeed they may enhance, your work and you will learn what suits you best.

8 Each half block alternates with a full block print, creating a 'stepped' silhouette into which subsequent blocks will fit, carrying on the overall flow of the design over the entire cloth. This is the customary way of arriving at a continuous overall hand-blocked design and is no harder to achieve once you grasp the purpose and can see the result. Printing the same block side by side, as in tiles, creates a quite different look, more naive, as in a medieval herbal, and without the sense of overall flow and movement. Try both on spare cloth for comparison.

9 Let the finished printed cloth dry, then finish as specified by the maker – some require ironing to fix the colour for washing. Tack and machine the hems all round.

PRINTED
WALLPAPER BORDERS

H ANDPRINTED BORDERS, using lino cuts, deliver something of the feistiness of an Edward Bawden print, and take less time than wallpaper both in the cutting of the block and in its handprinting. As ever, choose or devise a design appropriate to your medium; something vigorous and boldly readable from a distance is the thing to aim for. You can see from our examples how lively and colourful the results can be. Borders do not have to be en suite with wallpaper. In fact, borders as graphic as these would look more effective used alongside rich emulsion (latex) wall colours, rather than a patterned paper. Though the shops are stuffed with borders, I rarely find one gutsy enough. If this is your problem, too, it should encourage you to know that printing off a length of border to go round an average-sized room should not take more than a couple of hours. Cutting the block is extra. But not only will you be saving real money, your hand-blocked border will be unique.

YOU WILL NEED

A roll of lining paper
Lino block cut to size and mounted on
  chipboard
Lino cutting tools, 'V'- and 'U'-shaped gouges
Oil-based relief printing inks
White spirit (mineral spirits)
Scalpel, steel rule, pencil to mark and cut strips
Improvised printing table – kitchen table
  covered with an old blanket plus plastic
  sheet stapled or tacked to keep it flat
Roller
Piece of thick, bevelled glass
Palette knife

1 Warm the lino on a radiator to make it easier to cut. Transfer your design onto the block (cut to size) either via carbon paper or by scribbling over the back of your design paper with soft lead pencil.

2 Cut your design, first incising the outlines with the 'V'-shaped gouge, then changing to the 'U'-shaped tool to scrape away the background material.

3 Cut lining paper into manageable lengths, say, 10 feet (3 metres). Then mark off strips, using the steel rule and pencil, making sure they are all approximately half an inch (1.25 cm) wider than your block, to leave a small margin top and bottom when printing.

4 Make sure your printing table is taut and shipshape. If your kitchen table is not long enough, a large piece of MDF (medium density fibreboard) could be laid on top. Or set up a trestle table – these are not expensive and are endlessly useful. A flat surface is important for printing on. A painter's dustsheet or length of canvas could go over the old blanket, if you dislike plastic, but make sure the whole set-up is steady, the covering taut, tacked or stapled in place at strategic intervals.

5 Tack, weight or staple the cut strips onto your printing table. You will be able to print off several strips at one go.

6 Mix up the printing ink. Oil-based relief printing inks are sticky, so add a little white spirit (mineral spirits).

7 Use the roller to ink your block. Position the block so that a small margin of paper shows each side, then print off with hand pressure, or with a mallet if you have one. Re-ink the block and carry on. Take a little care over registering; noticeable gaps are better avoided, though you can always cut and rejoin the border when pasting up on the wall. Our design was planned to make registration easy, the snail shape slotting neatly into the half circle blank at the end of the previous print.

8 Leave the printed borders to dry off completely before pasting up.

STENCILS

THE ORIGINS OF THIS breathtakingly obvious solution to repeat pattern-making are lost far back in history, and probably antedate the remaining evidence. We know the Chinese and the Egyptians made use of stencils thousands of years ago, around the time of the Great Wall and the Pyramids. Their stencils were probably cut from leather, and their paints made of earth pigments bound with animal size, but they used them in the same way and for the same reasons that we do, for quick repeats. Anywhere you see repeats on a large scale in decoration, you may suspect the use of stencilling, often combined with freehand painting, to which the stencilling played a subsidiary role – powdering the background with gold stars, confining murals within a border, apprentice work. Which is not to say that stencilled decoration cannot look as rich and complex as a Persian emperor's prayer rug, or a piece of Chinese *cloisonné*. In late nineteenth-century Britain, Morris and Co. designed stencilled polychrome wall schemes of medieval inspiration, mostly for churches, of intense elaboration, with as many colours as William Morris's carpets and wallpapers. The most complicated repeat pattern can be replicated via stencils, provided you have the patience to cut a new stencil for every separate colour element in the design. Recently, the designer John Stefanides created a memorable stencilled wall scheme in colours inspired by a faded antique Indian palampore, or handpainted textile. Ambitious projects like these can employ a team of people for weeks, months even in the case of churches stencilled from narthex to altar, in several colours, embellished with gold leaf.

Our stencil projects, by comparison, are relatively undemanding of time and patience, though some care and perseverance is always required to cut a fine stencil, with slick, bevelled edges and a nice flow to the curves. They use every advance in photocopying technology for blowing up images, and the newest paint solutions to the problems of painting on fabrics, ceramic and glass. They are an encouraging glimpse into the potential for stencils to transform blank surfaces into something uniquely your own.

A ravishing patka *from Rajasthan, dating from the seventeenth to eighteenth century, shows the delicacy of stencilled pattern typical of the Indian master craftsman.*

THE TECHNIQUE

For those who haven't yet tried their hand at stencilling, a short re-cap on the process and its dos and don'ts seems indicated. Likely designs can be found in any library, and a small sketch or photograph enlarged to A4 size for a few pence. From this it is simple enough to trace off the design onto stencil card, which most experts prefer to acetate because it is so much easier to cut smoothly. Or, as shown below, you can eliminate one process by pasting the photocopy straight onto stencil card and cutting through both at once. For this we used a spray adhesive, Spraymount, which gives uniform adhesion with two quick puffs on the back of your photocopy. Most people use a scalpel, with a supply of new blades, for cutting, because it slices through card keenly and, being a precision tool, allows much greater control than a heavy Stanley knife. (Use pliers to change blades or you risk cuts.) Cutting should be done at a slight angle to create a bevelled edge, not straight down. The bevelled edge helps prevent paint 'creeping', while the angled cut makes for smoothness. Jags and scruffy edges can be tidied up with further cutting, or with fine sandpaper, but a clean-cut, handsome stencil is an inspiration to use.

It is always a good idea to paint your first stencil onto a spare sheet of card, as reference record and in case your first stencil disintegrates after much use. Using water-based paints, as most stencillers do, for their speedy drying and non-smudging qualities, does make traditional stencil card fall apart sooner, as moisture gets into the cut surfaces. This can be postponed by brushing over the completed, cut stencil with shellac. Small, compact stencils can be held in place while working with one's free hand. Larger, open-work stencils are best given a whiff of Spraymount on the back, which holds them in place but allows them to be peeled off and re-positioned. There was a vogue for stencilling with spray paints, but most decorators now agree these are more trouble than they are worth, because so much masking off is needed that it is quicker to use a brush and paint in the conventional way.

PAINTS

The advantages of fast-drying acrylic paints (water-based) have made them firm favourites with stencillers. It is, of course, possible to use almost any medium for stencilling, but acrylic-based colours have the huge merit of drying almost instantly, which makes smudging less likely as the card is removed; of being permanent (they don't require varnishing, except when applied to furniture); and of lending themselves to a range of effects, from almost transparent (when extended with Flow Enhancer) to crisply opaque. For a soft, faded look, attractive on some walls and on furniture decoration, we often use transparent water-based glazes, colourwash, for stencilling. Emulsion (latex) paints, sold in sample pots, can also be used for stencilling, and are popular, but to a critical eye they deliver a stodgy colour due to the ingredients designed to make them cover well. But the rule, whatever paint you use, is to take it up on the brush, pounce the bristles onto waste paper to blot up moisture, then stencil. A wet, overloaded brush will always produce a muzzy, smudgy stencil. The ideal to aim for is a crisp but delicate 'print', not a crude splodge. Sensitive 'shading' is easily done by over-brushing with a second colour, selectively.

BRUSHES

The traditional stencil brush is blunt cut, quite hard bristled, and used with a 'pouncing' motion, as in stippling. These still have their uses, but the action is tiring repeated over a large area, and an almost identical effect – crisp, delicate – can be arrived at using a round-headed stencil brush and working colour on in a round-and-round motion, like scrubbing at a stain. For this a next-to-dry brush is essential, or moisture will be deposited at the cut edges and leak when the stencil is lifted.

It is only fair to say that super carefulness is more a concern when stencilling on surfaces like furniture or fabrics which may come under close scrutiny, and where the stencil design predominates. Where a stencil is used repetitively on walls and the like, imperfections are lost in the overall effect. Indeed, some smudging or muzzy edges and variations in colour usually add a handmade charm to the final effect, over a large area, as in a hand-blocked print. You will inevitably find, if you tackle a large-scale project, that the work falls into a rhythm, the line of least resistance, dictated by impatience and fatigue. Obviously this should not be pushed to such extremes as blots, smudges and tears, but it teaches you as nothing else can the fastest route to the best effect, which is the driving force behind this ancient form of mass-production.

STENCILLED
MUSLIN CURTAINS

T HE DESIGN HERE, of a gently curving stem and slender, elegant leaves, was found in a botanical illustration and enlarged on a photocopier to a size that would 'read' at a glance when stencilled onto a plain white cotton muslin to make fresh, translucent curtains. The motif is strong enough to possess the fabric, even with plenty of white space around, and lively and delicate enough to stand repetition without monotony. It has an affinity with some of William Morris's designs, like the famous Willow, and yet, through its sparse execution, evokes the mood of later designers such as Charles Rennie Mackintosh. And, to be practical, such a large motif, well spaced, will deliver the goods for much less time and effort than something small and intricate. It is worth bearing in mind while you are photocopying that it is sensible to make at least a dozen photocopies of your chosen image, as this makes planning the finished design much faster and easier.

YOU WILL NEED

Lengths of white muslin
Several photocopies of your motif
Large sheet of stencil card
Spraymount (*see* p. 192)
Scalpel plus blades
Red felt-tip pen for registration marks
Fabric paint
Stencil brushes, medium and small
Wax plate palette
Masking tape

1 Begin by laying out your photocopied images on stencil card to determine spacing, direction, etc. This was seen as a continuous pattern of fronds, uncurling gracefully, with a change of direction from one line to the next, left to right then right to left. It could all have been done with one stencil, but for speed, being a relatively simple stencil to cut, it seemed sensible to cut a whole 'repeat', with six images cut on the same stencil. This saves time with such tasks as measuring and registering, which becomes important over a long piece of cloth.

3 The completed stencil, taking up a whole sheet of card, appears as the last photocopy is peeled off. At this point, work out where repeats should fall, both horizontally and vertically, and mark with a red felt-tip pen on the stencil card.

2 When the design is determined, Spray-mount photocopies on the back and press down to stick to the stencil card. Using the scalpel, cut through photocopy and stencil card, leaving 'bridges' (*see* p. 192) as necessary to hold the motif together. Repeat with all motifs.

4 A willow-green fabric paint is prepared on the palette, mixing paint colours as necessary to achieve the right shade.

5 Stencilling in progress, showing how the brush strokes colour through the cut-out motif onto the fabric below. The fabric and card should be spread out on a large flat surface for this, and the stencil fixed into position with tabs of masking tape or pins.

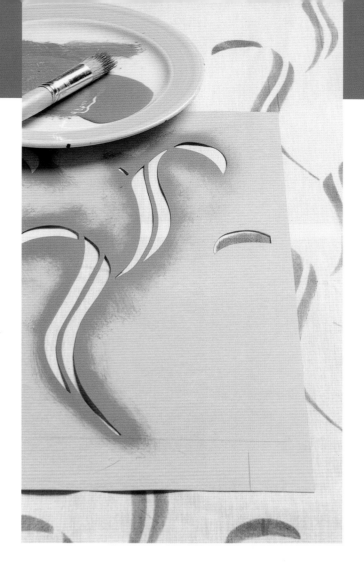

6 After one 'block' of stencils is completed, the card is moved up (or across) using the registration marks to position it accurately for the next repeat. Regular spacing is important for the flow of this design, so the 'tails' of the second block of motifs descend between the fronds of the first to the same level established on the 'master' stencil. The same holds true when moving the stencil across a wide fabric. Use registration marks to ensure the next block of motifs is evenly spaced, and parallel, and on the same horizontal.

7 The finished fabric, humble muslin newly transformed into a subtle and appealing print with a springlike feel, and a sinuous and lively movement of delicate green shapes.

FISH & CHIPSDISH

IT IS RATHER WONDERFUL to think that run-of-the-mill items of catering china, like the flat white serving dish and the bowl here, can be turned into something as witty and attractive as our Fish and Chips project. I can see this as the start of a whole suite of china, using smaller fish. Just the thing for Mediterranean-style salads and, naturally, fish dishes to be eaten outside on a hot day. Almost as wonderful is the fact that the ceramic paint used can be made dishwasher proof by simply warming it up in the oven for 45 minutes.

The technique here uses a template for the elegant fishy skeletons, a sort of 'reverse' or 'positive' stencil, and a stencil proper for the chips. Another departure from the usual stencil process is that the colour is applied with a natural sponge, which is fun and quick, and gives the design much of its breezy charm.

YOU WILL NEED

Ceramic 'blank' (from catering suppliers)
Liquitex Glossies acrylic enamels in bright blue
  and yellow (*see* p. 191)
Natural sponge   Pencil
Greaseproof paper   Spraymount
Scalpel

1 The fish skeleton was drawn onto blue greaseproof paper doubled over and cut out with a scalpel, to make two fish templates. Ordinary paper would not be suitable because the sponging would soak it. But a sheet of acetate would do instead.

2 After a bit of experimenting to find the best arrangement for the dish, the templates were given a whiff of Spraymount on the backs and pressed down smoothly on the dish.

3 Using a small sea sponge, dipped in blue acrylic enamel, the outside of the dish was lightly pounced with colour just as far as the sloping rim, fading the sponging out towards the perimeter. To prevent colour straying, an oval of grease-proof was cut, using the dish as a pattern, to fit over the rim, and held down as sponging pro-gressed. Masking tape would do the same job.

4 Peeling away the template reveals the fish skeleton in negative, white against its Mediterranean blue background. The second fish was sponged the same way, shifting the greaseproof collar round to the other side.

5 A series of chip shapes were cut round the outside of the greaseproof collar, given a touch of Spraymount to hold the paper steady, and then sponged over with bright yellow, adjusting the oval cut-out to fit the shape and curve of the dish.

6 To make the enamel waterproof, the dish was put in a cold oven, which was then set at 160°C (325°F) and left for approximately 45 minutes, to bake the enamel decoration.

ETCHED GLASS
WINDOW

E TCHED GLASS has been undergoing a serious revival, for its decorativeness, for the privacy it gives and for its usefulness in blocking off unlovely views. Stencilling with Frosting Medium gives much the same effect at a fraction of the cost, with the bonus that you don't need to remove and re-glaze the window. It is a particularly nice touch, when working on a small paned window as here, to fit the stencil to the glass panes, easily done by enlarging or reducing the design on a photocopier. Look for suitable designs in your local library. Ours derives from a design for ornamental ironwork, the sort of template you may find in old architectural pattern books.

YOU WILL NEED

Photocopied motif
Stencil card
Spraymount
Scalpel and blades
Frosting Medium (*see* p. 191)
White acrylic or emulsion paint (optional)

1 The photocopied design, enlarged to size, is fixed to card with Spraymount, and cut through with a scalpel.

2 As the photocopy is removed, crisp bevelled edges are revealed: this is high-class cutting.

3 Frosting Medium (add a touch of white acrylic or emulsion if you want privacy more than translucency) is stippled through the stencil onto each glass pane in turn. At first it appears almost water clear, but it becomes cloudy, like etched glass, as it dries and hardens.

4 The finished window, is translucently pretty, yet gives privacy without loss of light. Windows should be thoroughly cleaned prior to stencilling, and wiped over gently rather than scoured in the future. The Frosting Medium is surprisingly tough, but obviously not as durable as real etched glass.

PARQUETRYFLOOR

A CRISP, GEOMETRIC STENCIL like the one shown here makes a brilliantly effective, as well as pleasingly thrifty, disguise for floorboards which have seen better days, a cement screed too horrible to live with, or the sheets of plywood or hardboard which turn up sometimes under the decaying cork tiles, repulsive carpeting, and all the rest of the unsatisfactory cut-price solutions to the daunting problem of what to do about the floors. Painting your floor is a very nineties answer to that, now that word has got out that they are surprisingly durable, a total disguise for what's there, and can look as handsome as anything on the market costing at least twenty times more. Don't think of painting over a decent floor – oak boards, parquet, Norwegian pine and the like. But as a speedy remedy for sub-standard flooring, this is the smart solution. Warmth underfoot can be supplied with the odd rug, or mat. We devised a *trompe-l'oeil* design to initiate a standard pattern of inlaid wood – parquetry.

Existing floors need to be prepped beforehand, washed or scrubbed to remove grease and nasties. A light sanding could be helpful, to give a clean surface for paint, but is not essential. On boards, nails will need punching down, and any grievous damage must be filled with plastic wood. Basically, surfaces, whether wood, concrete, plywood or hardboard, should be clean, dry, with enough 'tooth' to bond with paint. We generally use standard emulsion (latex), which is fast drying and covers well, using varnish – several coats of acrylic, quick-drying varnish – to give protection underfoot. A first coat of acrylic primer makes your paint go further. It dries in less than half an hour.

YOU WILL NEED

Acrylic primer
Sage green emulsion (latex) as base coat
  (or whatever you choose)
Dark green and white emulsion (latex) for
  stencilling

Stencil brushes
Stencil card
Scalpel
Spraymount

Pencil
Masking tape
Steel measuring tape
Acrylic floor varnish

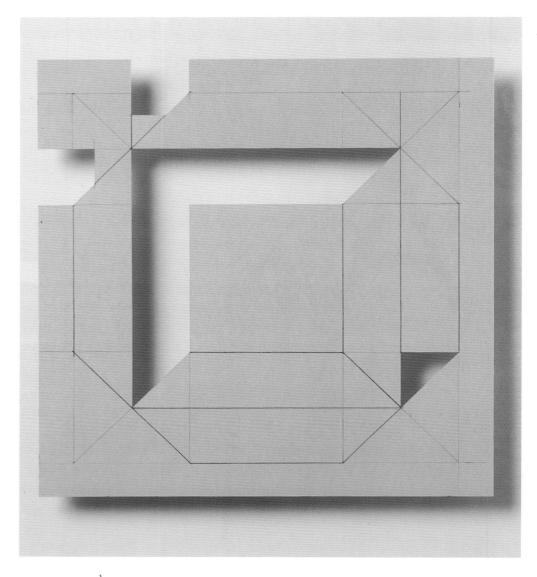

2 Paint entire floor with one coat acrylic primer followed by two coats emulsion (latex) base colour. These can be applied by roller. Let them dry well in between.

3 Transfer design for stencil to card, as previously described, using Spraymount to fix design in place and cutting through both simultaneously. If the floor is large, you might be better off using clear acetate, or mylar, which is extra tough and can be cut in clean geometric shapes quite easily. Otherwise, make two stencils.

1 Measure floor area and mark out on squared paper, to scale, to determine how many repeats you will need of a design approximately 12 inches (30 cm) square. Few rooms are exactly symmetrical, walls bulge in or out, right angles are not precisely 90 degrees. A plain painted border takes care of these variations neatly. Here we simply left a strip of the base paint colour all round the space, adding a dark inset strip, 2 inches (5 cm) wide to mark off the stencilled area.

4 Using your squared paper plan as guide, check quickly how many repeats will fit into your space. I usually find it easiest to chalk guidelines across the space in both directions, bisecting the centre of the floor.

5 This design uses two stencils, one for the dark right-angled border, another simple square for the 'middles'. The remaining two sides of the 'frame' are supplied by the base colour.

6 With Stencil 1, the two dark sides to the 'frame', use a whiff of Spraymount on the back to secure, position according to your floor plan, then stencil, using very little paint – an almost dry brush. Pounce surplus moisture/paint off onto newspaper first, if in doubt.

7 Stencil 2, the square for the white paint, slots between the arms of Stencil 1. You can stencil this as you go along, which makes registration quicker, or complete all Stencil 1 process, then fill in with Stencil 2. The paint dries very fast, but even so, try to avoid crawling over recently stencilled areas.

8 Carry on till the whole floor area is patterned. Let dry overnight if possible. Then varnish two or three times with a quick drying (20–30 minutes) acrylic floor varnish, leaving several hours hardening time in between.

SCREEN PRINTING

STENCILLING AND SILK SCREEN printing link together quite naturally, since the one is simply an extension of the possibilities of the other. Both are about the rapid multiplication of motifs or designs over a wide variety of surfaces, using stencils, or cut-outs, for the purpose. Stencilling is a manual operation, and therefore both slower and more laborious, but it offers greater freedom of application. A stencil can be used to create repeat patterns on walls, ceilings, floors, furniture, fabric, any surface that can be reached by a hand holding a brush. Materials for silk screening, on the other hand, must be fastened into a frame before colour is forced through the stencil with a squeegee, to make a print. While silk screening can be used to print a good variety of surfaces – fabric, paper, glass, wood, rubber, metal and so forth – its use is clearly restricted to materials that can be laid flat in a frame under pressure. However, once the frame and stencil are set up for silk screen printing, endless replicas of an image can be turned out with little effort.

There is a professional slickness to a screen print that glorifies and adds value, visually, to the simplest of designs using the humblest of materials. Our demonstration of screen printing techniques illustrates this beautifully. Its stylish pattern, a sort of irregular mosaic in tawny yellow on a deep, glowing orange ground, was created from nothing more elaborate than a handful of scraps of torn paper, artistically disposed. The screen used was a small one, so to arrive at a fabric square large enough to cover a decent sized cushion, we decided to print four identical designs separated by a wavy margin of unprinted natural calico. The margin was created by using

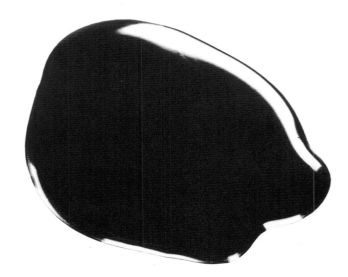

more torn paper to form the edges of the first print, which consisted of solid blocks of orange positioned to make up an equidistant foursome on the fabric square. This necessitated a fair bit of masking off, since the silk screen frame was rectangular and the orange blocks are square.

The other problem we encountered was the one endemic to printing repeats, which is registration. It mattered that the mosaic pattern was centred precisely on its orange block each time. The simple solution to this was to make the first pull of the mosaic design onto a sheet of tracing paper, wavy edges, torn paper scraps and all. This provided a handy 'master' for positioning the orange blocks each time so that the mosaic would fall into place, correctly aligned.

If this sounds complicated, the answer is that what might seem long-winded to print four screen printed blocks begins to make sense if you print off hundreds at a time, which most people, given the simplicity of the actual printing process, would normally be contemplating. However, the up side of this (and it may come as a revelation to people looking at screen printing for the first time) is the delightful simplicity of assembling the design itself. The mosaic design was not cut as a stencil. Instead, the scraps of torn paper were scattered about on one of the printed orange blocks until the arrangement looked satisfying, then the frame was closed, the screen inked, and lo and behold the scraps of paper fastened themselves obligingly to the screen, creating the mosaic 'master' through which subsequent 'pulls' could be made over and over again, as the orange blocks were over-printed with deep red. This fortuitous behaviour of the silk screen process is one that professionals are well aware of and obviously adds to its appeal, since it exploits a random and creative characteristic of what is, finally, a mechanical and repetitive process.

You may prefer, in the end, to use cut stencils for your screen printing, and you may not begrudge the time it takes to cut different stencils for each colour inking and printing. But it is helpful to start with an open mind and a grasp of the shortcuts available, because time finally equals money, unless you are purely investigating the technique for your private interest and amusement. Speedy results are the only way a more commercial approach can work, in my experience – employing a trick in the process which looks more than it is. And of course it is sobering to remind yourself just how many people are even now researching the decorative field for exactly these impressive shortcuts.

Our scrap paper mosaic idea is precisely the sort of breezy solution that could turn the corner for a cottage industry and put it into the black. The screen printing process makes it look more complicated than it is. The idea itself is worth developing and revolving and experimenting with, a seed which can be grown and manipulated, cleverly, into a full-blown design all your own.

YOU WILL NEED

Screen printing frame
Squeegee (*see* p. 192)
Nylon mesh for screen
Ochre and red Ocaldo
  (*see* p. 191) water-
  based inks
Paper
Masking tape

1 The first step, after fastening the nylon mesh in place across the frame to provide the screen, is to arrange strips of torn masking tape round the underside of the screen to make a wavy-edged square through which the four orange blocks are printed.

2 More masking tape is used to cut down the size of the screen from a rectangle to a square.

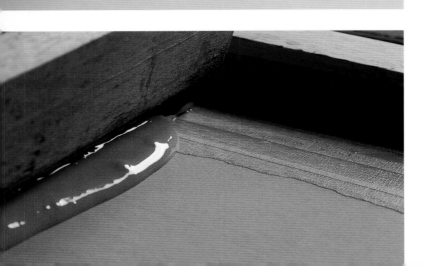

3 The fabric has been positioned on the baseboard, the frame lowered in place and screwed down with wing nuts either side, and the ochre ink is puddled at the hinged end of the screen. The squeegee is then used to pull it the length of the screen, forcing the ink through the wavy-edged square, or improvised stencil, on the underside of the screen. The squeegee is held at both ends and drawn towards and then away from the operator, to ensure the paint has covered, with firm, decisive strokes.

4 The screen is raised, showing the first pull – a bright ochre square on the calico. This process is repeated four times in all, to print off the four ochre blocks that make up the basis of our design. As the cloth is moved for each square, newspaper is laid over the damp printed areas to protect them from smudging on the screen.

5 On the second pull the squeegee is drawn in the reverse direction, to make use of surplus ink from the first 'pull'. Surplus ink is then removed with a palette knife, and the screen washed clean in hot water. A new masking tape border is then stuck down before the next printing stage.

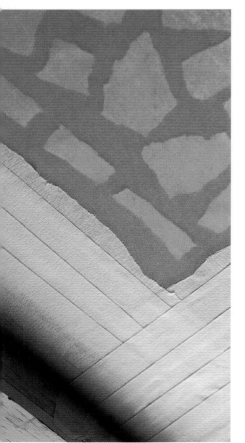

6 Scraps of torn paper are arranged over the last printed square, still in place on the baseboard, to make a pleasing, irregular mosaic. The frame is closed and the squeegee given a further pass over the screen. This leaves the paper scraps fixed to the screen to make the 'stencil' for the second stage of the design.

7 The first 'pull' in the second colour, a bright red, is onto a sheet of tracing paper. The purpose of this is to serve as a guide to positioning the orange blocks for over-printing in red.

8 The tracing paper print is used to line up the second block of colour for over-printing in red. The first overprint is shown here on the left, which gives the effect of an orange yellow mosaic on a deep crimson background.

9 The process is repeated, over-printing all four blocks in red to give the design shown in our final photograph, a vivid print of mosaic blocks separated by wavy margins of the original calico.

TIGERANDZEBRA
CUSHIONS

A LARGER SCREEN WAS USED FOR THIS DESIGN, so that each print was big enough to cover a cushion. The design was made by a process of deliberate doodling, often recommended as a way to loosen up the design of a screen print. A pencil was used to make sweeping diagonal curving lines, irregular in shape and size but all following the same flowing movement and direction. The result is much like tiger stripes. The zebra stripes were made by tearing out strips of paper in the freehand style of the squares shown in the description of the silk screen technique. The fabric squares were first printed in a base colour, beige in one case, cream in the other. This gives a sharper image and more contrast than would have been achieved by simply printing the stripes onto plain calico. Though the results are so striking, this was an altogether quicker screen printing process than that used for the orange and red squares above.

YOU WILL NEED

Calico
Screen printing frame and mesh
Squeegee
Beige, cream and black water-based inks
Pencil
Paper
Scalpel

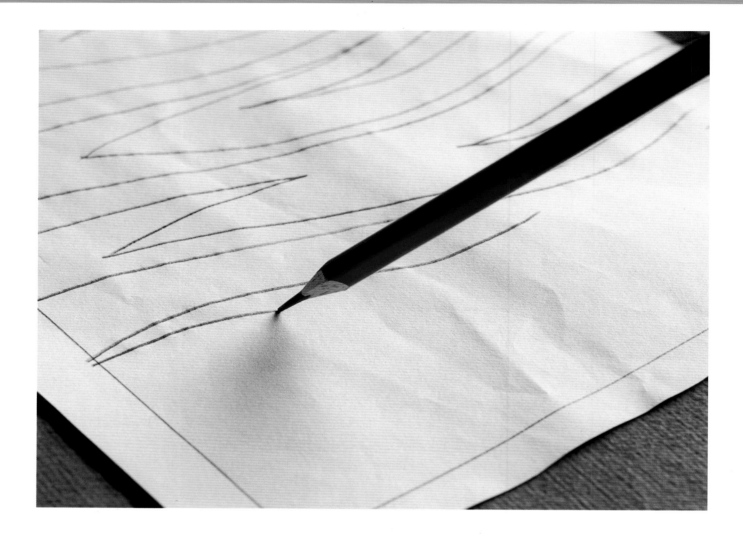

1 The calico was first printed with the base colours for our design, one beige square, one cream-coloured one. A good margin of fabric was left round each square, as a seam allowance when making up the cushions.

2 The screen was well washed between pulls. This is easily done now that water-based inks have superseded oil-based ones. The frame is held under a cold running tap and gently brushed to clear it of ink completely. A fan heater was used to dry the screen rapidly before re-inking.

3 This shows the tiger design taking shape on a sheet of paper. It may take several trial runs to arrive at a design as striking and balanced as this. Don't be afraid to play with different 'doodles'.

4 The finished design is cut out with a scalpel. This will serve as the stencil through which black ink is pushed with the squeegee to print the stripes onto the previously printed squares. The cut-out shapes will print black.

5 The cushion fabric squares were stretched over the baseboard one after another, the cut stencils laid on top, the frame closed and the screen inked in black this time. The squeegee was used as before, pulling the ink up the first time, down the next. After the first pull, the tiger stencil remained attached to the underside of the screen, as before.

SPONGE STAMPS

SPONGE STAMPS are the most recent innovation in the field of decorative printing. In fact, I would pin-point the birth of the idea as the early 1990s. One minute we were all experimenting with sponges for stencilling and for sponging colour on and off. And then, as if by osmosis, the notion of cutting cellulose sponge into decorative stamps struck several decorative painters almost simultaneously. I cut my first successful sponge stamp, a simple rosette, from neoprene, the dense soft rubbery substance used for wet suits. We have used a similar material for the stamps shown in this section because it is easier to cut smoothly than the standard cellulose sponges, which tend to be loose-textured and full of holes. Cutting these is rather like trying to carve a fresh loaf of bread – frustrating.

Sponge stamps are light and pleasant to use, and most uniformly printed by applying the colour to the sponge with a brush or roller. Dabbbing the stamp direct into a palette of colour will produce a cruder effect, which might nevertheless be what is wanted for some designs. I foresee sponge stamps taking off as more people discover how quick and cheap they are to make, and how easy to use for adding a bit of colour and pattern around the place. Sponge needs to be quite thick – three-quarters of an inch – to make a stand-alone stamp, as shown here. Thinner material like neoprene needs a backing of wood (like a lino cut) to keep it flat and to allow you to apply pressure evenly.

Start with simple motifs. The house and the building block are easy to carve, the rooster rather more difficult. Curves are more testing to cut than straight lines. A scalpel, with refill blades, is the only tool needed for cutting. Cut deliberately and slowly; don't hack. And remember that, as with any printing block or stamp, the printed image will be the mirror image of the one on your stamp. The rooster faces to the left on the stamp, for instance, but the printed rooster will face to the right. If you wanted to print two roosters facing each other, you would need to carve two stamps, one facing to the left and the other to the right. This may sound obvious but it is a point sometimes overlooked, to the subsequent discomfiture of the stamper.

*These vibrantly tinted liquids, on sale in a Sri Lankan shop, are
startling evidence of the intensity of natural dye colours.*

BUILDING BLOCK
DESIGN TRAY

A NITTY-GRITTY, simple motif based on a favourite patchwork design, known as building or tumbling blocks is used for a small wooden tray. The motif is so called because of the way the design, viewed from different angles, acquires a baffling 3-D perspective. All these designs derive, unexpectedly perhaps, from those for marble pavements by the Italian Renaissance architect Sebastiano Serlio (1475–1564), published in his treatises on architecture. From certain angles, these marble floors give an unsettling impression that you are about to step out onto a surface which is anything but flat, which seems to have been the Renaissance idea of a joke, and certainly had to do with their preoccupation with the laws of perspective. The idea translates well for a tray, an object also meant first and foremost to be flat and reliable.

YOU WILL NEED

Sponge material (we used neoprene and
    upholstery foam)
Photocopied images
Spraymount
Scalpel and spare blades
Kitchen towel
Emulsion (latex) paint
Acrylic artists' colours
PVA
Masking tape
Acrylic varnish

1 The photocopied motif is attached by Spraymount to the sponge block, previously cut to fit, and the design is then carved through paper and sponge simultaneously. This speeds things up, but if you find it difficult, trace or draw the design in white chalk pencil on the black sponge instead.

2 Use the scalpel to cut round the design first, then to pare away the background to leave the motif in relief. Thus, here, the central dot, outlines and two faces of the block are left in relief, while the area surrounding the dot (that is, anything that reads background white finally) is cut away.

3 Acrylic artists' colour is squeezed onto a plate and mixed with a tablespoon or so of PVA to give a translucent quality. The tray itself is painted with a base of white emulsion (latex).

4 The block is dipped gently into the paint mixture and tested on kitchen towel before printing the tray.

5 The 'blocks' being printed, side by side, using a piece of masking tape on the back as an improvised handle. With an interlocking design like this, registration is straightforward. Should a gap appear, touch it in with a brush. After printing, the tray is given two coats of acrylic varnish.

HOUSE AND ROOSTER WALLBLOCKING

TWO SMALL BLOCKS, of a stylized house and a splendidly feisty rooster, were used here to build up a highly decorative printed surface. This did not take long to do, despite the density of the design, but it would be a patient soul who chose to use it on a wall scale, unless it was printed up as a wallpaper! The completed design has a verve reminiscent of folk painting, though the choice of colours and the stepped grid lend it a greater sophistication. Both designs would also make splendid tile motifs, or centrepieces to a set of plates printed with the Liquitex Glossies mentioned in connection with stencilling techniques (*see* p. 136). Sponge stamps would be better suited to printing on shiny ceramic surfaces than lino cuts, and considerably faster than stencils. This is the sort of project children would enjoy. You could supply them with a box of plain white tiles, the cut stamps and paints, and leave them to make a set of bathroom tiles. Better to cut the stamps for them, however, as scalpels are not safe around children.

YOU WILL NEED

House and rooster stamps cut from thick black foam, as before
Roller
Coloured emulsion (latex) paints for printing (we used sap green and pale brick red)
PVA
Off-white emulsion paint for background
Buff colourwash (*see* p. 191)
Softening brush
Steel rule, pencil for measuring up grid

1 The background was first painted with off-white emulsion, and colourwashed in buff, using the softening brush to smooth out the glaze. A steel rule was used to measure an evenly spaced grid the width of a block apart: pencil point marks were made to indicate the top left-hand corner of each area to be stamped.

2 The house and the rooster stamps are cut from thick black foam with a sharp scalpel. The rooster, with its curves and feathers, demands greater cutting skills than the straight lines of the house.

3 The emulsion (latex) colours used for printing were spooned onto plates, and slightly thinned with water with a little PVA added to it, to speed drying and help the paint bond well.

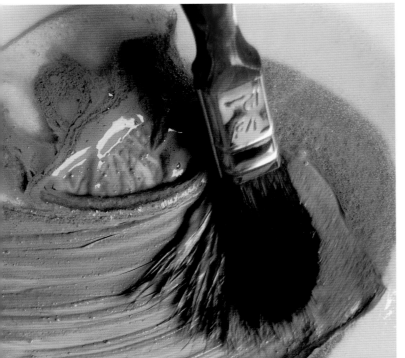

4 A roller was used to apply the colours to the stamps. This ensures an even coating of colour. On this porous surface brushed colour would be liable to go on patchily and print unevenly.

5 The same process was repeated with the rooster, so that the two blocks could be printed off alternately, using the pencil guidelines to keep the horizontals steady. Some people might prefer to print off a complete grid with one block in the same colour before filling in the spaces with the other. If you do this, remember to position the second row of prints between those on the row above.

STAMPED
BATHROOM**BORDER**

A STAMPED BORDER adds a nice finishing touch to bathroom walls colourwashed to shoulder height in a vivid Mediterranean blue. Patterned borders make very effective substitutes for traditional wooden dado rails, a visual trick that can make high ceilings look less lofty as well as adding colour and character to a functional bathroom space. The stamp for this print was cut from a softer, but less squidgy upholstery foam, which performed well, though it might be helpful to stick it to a rigid backing if you are stamping a large area. Cut the backing (plywood, rigid plastic) with sides on the diagonal, following the sloping sides of the motif. This will make accurate registration of the design much easier, since the tip of each 'tail' can be positioned under the nick in the tail above, as our pictures show. The horizontal lines enclosing the border can either be cut *en suite* with the motif or painted in by hand afterwards, using the trick with double strips of masking tape to keep them straight, unless you prefer them a little wavy, as we have made them here.

The wall here was first painted out with white non-absorbent colourwash base, a product which helps to keep the water-based glaze open for as long as possible while you brush out the wet colour with a softening brush to give as much or little colour as you fancy. The same blue colourwash, with a little PVA added for strength and 'stick', was used to print the border, giving a soft, attractive print with lots of colour and texture variation. Printing with transparent colour gives quite different effects from printing with opaque colour, an ethereal quality which can be exploited for its own contribution to the overall look of a design.

YOU WILL NEED

Length of upholstery foam	Roller and artist's brush	Wallpaper paste
Scalpel and spare blades	Colourwash base	PVA
Photocopied design	Colourwash (*see* p. 191)	Colourwash matt acrylic varnish
Spraymount		Masking tape

1 Use Spraymount to fix the photocopy to the foam and cut through both at once. The walls here were given a base coat of Regency White colourwash base, and then painted with Mediterranean Blue colourwash, applied loosely for a Mediterranean watery look. A strip of masking tape marked the line for the stamped border and the upper limit of colourwash.

2 Once the colour-wash had dried (4–8 hours) on the walls, more of the same colourwash was tipped onto a plate and mixed with a little PVA and a couple of tablespoons of wallpaper paste. After testing the colour on paper we found it too strong, so more paste was mixed in too.

3 The masking tape was peeled off the walls, then the cut sponge, which is an update on a classical scroll pattern, was brushed over with the colourwash mix described, tested for consistency of the print on a piece of newspaper, and then pressed firmly along the wall, using the colourwash tide-mark as a guideline.

4 Bathrooms need more wiping down than most places, so the whole wall surface was given a couple of coats of a fast-drying matt acrylic varnish designed to go over colourwashed finishes.

FOUNDOBJECTS

F OUND AND FORTUITOUS OBJECTS have always played a part in printing and pattern-making, from earliest times. Handprints are an obvious example; the use of leaves, shells or cereals to impress designs into potters' clay, another. Primitive people had limited resources, compared with ourselves, but they used them with skill and imagination to achieve satisfying and sometimes beautiful results. This section of the book is designed to stretch the imagination a little by showing what can be done with the unlikeliest materials if you keep your eyes and mind open. There is a quite special pleasure to be found in exercising one's resourcefulness, not so much because it is gratifying to make something out of nothing, but because it encourages you to look about you in a freshly creative way.

Sati hand-prints executed in mud relief and set into a façade of the Jodhpur Palace, Rajasthan, India.

173

WOODBLOCK CHAIR**COVER**

BALSA WOOD, that weightless, easily cut friend of the model maker, lends itself to very rapid, painless printing blocks, as long as you respect the grain of the material, which cuts very readily into straight lines and geometric shapes, but is apt to splinter off if you attempt curves and twiddly bits. The designs we chose were a dead simple grid of parallel lines and another of squares, which were easy to cut and construct. But, as the results show, 'building block' types of motifs like these can deliver very stylish patterns. However, it is wise to rough out the overall design first, so you know what you are aiming for. The diagonal lines which give interest to the prints are an attractive bonus of working with grained wood. This is probably about as far as you can go with added detail when using this material. We used our finished fabric to upholster a simple dining chair, which instantly becomes a grander, hand-crafted piece of furniture.

YOU WILL NEED

Balsa wood blocks and half-inch (1.25 cm) strips
Piece of chipboard as backing board
Pencil
Scalpel with spare blades
Wood-bonding glue
Emulsion paint or fabric printing paint (we used a
    dark blue and an ochre yellow)
Roller or brush
Tack hammer
Drawing pins or staple gun
Fabric for printing

1 Use pencil to draw the design of four squares onto the balsa wood block.

2 Using scalpel blade, cut through the balsa wood block to approximately quarter inch or half centimetre depth, following the tracing or pencil lines. Scrape out any spare material to leave the design in clear relief.

3 Construct the second printing block by arranging three evenly spaced lines of balsa strips at right angles to each other, glued to the chipboard backing.

4 Stretch fabric onto a padded surface (we used a blanket), and secure with drawing pins or staples to keep it as taut as possible.

5 Use roller or brush to ink the balsa wood blocks, testing on paper first. When printing, a firm impression from the block can be made by applying a sharp tap with the hammer on the back of each block.

OMEGA LEAF
STAMP

W HAT COULD BE MORE HUMDRUM than a roll of draught excluder? The idea of using it to make an outsize stamp was a sudden brainwave. It grew out of thinking about something fairly pliable, soft and three-dimensional, like rope but not rope; and via one of those quirky mental leaps, the answer came pat – draught excluder. It is less pliable than I remembered, but usefully self-adhesive one side and squashy the other.

The leaf design, by the Omega Workshops out of Matisse, evolved from experimenting with the material itself, which seemed to lend itself to a big, bold, fluid shape. The stamp was so successful we decided to dramatize it with a really funky colour scheme, shades of blue against a glowing orange. Orange emulsion tends to look harsh. We used a reddish colourwash over an orange emulsion base to give an orange with depth, vibrant but not hard. The leaf shape was traced round to make an outsize stencil, and we used this to brush leaf shapes randomly and every whichway in a light chalky blue. The blue stencil colour was applied loosely, leaving some of the orange base showing through. Then the leaf stamp was used to print dark blue outlines over the stencilled motifs.

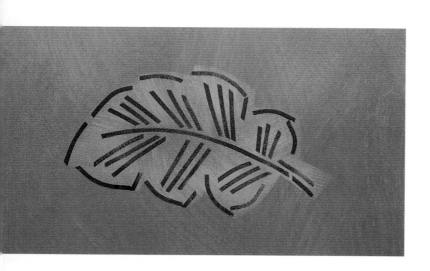

The resulting design seemed worth the trouble of this sequence of painting, but a boldly graphic effect could be achieved much more rapidly by simply printing the leaf outline in a strongly contrasting colour over an existing emulsion base. Vary the effect by changing the angle of your print, but remember that this stamp is directional – the movement is from left to right. If you want the balance of a leaf going in the opposite direction, you will need to make a second stamp. This could be a smaller leaf, differently shaped, or an identical twin facing the other way; or you could add a completely different motif.

YOU WILL NEED

One roll draught excluder tape
Stiff card or thin plywood for backing
Scalpel and spare blades
Pencil
Printing colour
Stencil paint/emulsion/colourwash as necessary
Stencil brush/stencil card
Soft brush/roller

If colourwashing, apply over emulsion (latex)
  base according to printed instructions.

3 Brush chalky blue stencil paint loosely – that is, not too carefully and solidly – through the leaf stencil where your eye dictates, fairly evenly spaced, but pointing in different directions. Make sure to brush in away from the edge of the stencil, so that the border of the print is unsmudged. Unless you have made a second stamp, facing the other way, make sure your leaf stencils all face the same way as the stamp, or you will be in trouble. Stencils can be reversed, but not stamps.

1 Draw out leaf shape on card or plywood and cut out with scalpel or a jigsaw.

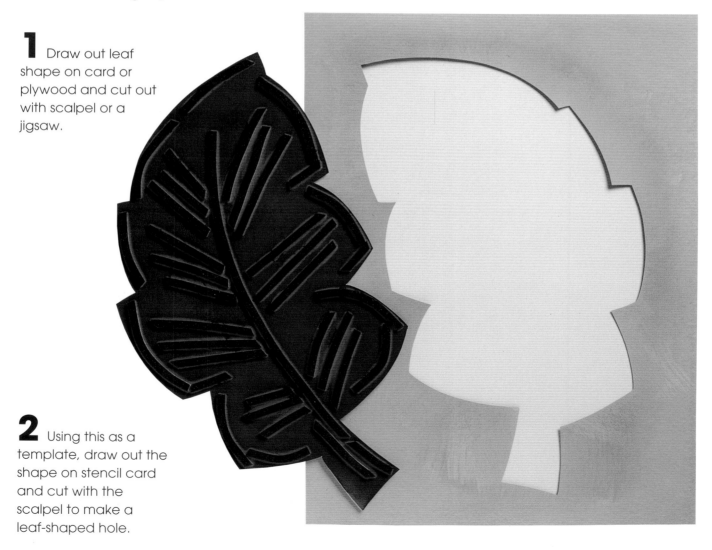

2 Using this as a template, draw out the shape on stencil card and cut with the scalpel to make a leaf-shaped hole.

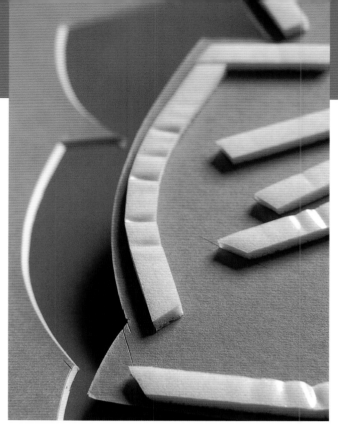

4 Use draught excluder tape, sticky side down, to build up the leaf outline and veining on the card or plywood backing. Tight curves cannot be formed from the tape intact, so cutting and joining pieces is needed here. When the pattern is complete, remove the thin plastic coating from the top side of the tape, easing up its edge with a scalpel.

5 Brush or roll printing colour over the completed stamp, and press firmly down over the stencilled shapes already painted on the wall. Use both hands to distribute pressure evenly. Repeat, re-colouring each time.

THE **ROPE**TRICK

A LENGTH OF ROPE, being flexible but stoutly textured, makes another 'found' printing material with decorative potential. The weave and texture of rope become attractively apparent in a print. It struck us as an appropriate material for printing onto something similarly sturdy, like a canvas deckchair cover. Canvas curtains would look good, too, scattered widely with a bold motif like our free-form star shape, as would robust floor cushions. Keep to loosely structured, large-scale motifs which can be easily formed with soft rope, and make sure you glue up any cut ends of the rope to stop the fibres unravelling and spoiling the design.

YOU WILL NEED

Length of soft cotton rope
Emulsion (latex) paint
PVA
Small roller
Square of thin plywood, or stiff card, for backing
Impact adhesive
Canvas material

1 Work out the approximate size and form of your design, and cut a square of plywood or stiff card as backing for the 'rope trick'. Use impact adhesive to glue the rope motif in place onto the backing, and to hold all the cut ends neatly together.

2 Spoon your chosen emulsion colour, adding a little PVA as reinforcement binder, onto a flat surface. With your roller, apply the paint over the surface of the rope motif. Test on a sheet of brown paper before starting on the fabric.

3 Decide where you want to position the motif, then lay the canvas on a table or other flat surface padded with newspaper.

4 Print off the rope motif, using steady pressure all over the backing. Some people use a mallet, others a rolling-pin, but firm hand pressure is adequate.

A **NUTTY**PROJECT

IMPRESSING IS A PART of the letterpress process, where metal type is brought into contact with paper in a hand, or machine, press (*see* p. 10). We decided to adapt the idea loosely with three-dimensional shapes – walnut, brazil and hazlenut (cob) shells – impressed into a clay base retained in a temporary wooden frame. A runny plaster of Paris mix was poured into the 'mould'. When dry, the frame was taken to pieces to reveal a chunky plaster frame decorated with a nutty bas-relief. Some of the earliest printing, in Mexico, was done with baked clay cylinders, so there is a real link with letterpress from an early date. We liked its plastery plainness, but it would have lent itself to gilding, or antiquing with paint washes followed by antiquing wax, or dark boot polish, to enhance the 3-D modelling.

YOU WILL NEED

Lengths of thin plywood for the frame
Well-wedged potter's clay
Rolling-pin
A roll of orthopaedic bandage (or length of
   scrim or hessian cut into strips)
Plaster of Paris
Plastic buckets
Brazilnuts, walnuts and hazlenuts
Strong sticky tape

1 First wedge your clay thoroughly, till malleable and to remove air bubbles. Roll into a long cylinder. Cut into four equal lengths, for a square frame, or two longer, two shorter for a rectangular frame.

2 Use a rolling-pin to flatten the lengths of clay, equally. Lay out in a frame shape and join the four corners with firm pressure, smoothing afterwards to keep them even. It is easier to press the relief design into the clay base before assembling the mould.

3 The various nuts were pushed into the still malleable clay to leave clear impressions, thickly spaced together. The nuts were moved round to give a variety of impressions.

4 A temporary form, or mould, made of lengths of plywood cut to enclose the clay base, was assembled round the impressed clay frame. The ply was taped at the corners to hold it together, using strong sticky tape, and the seams here and at the base sealed with lumps of clay to make the mould watertight.

5 A runny mix of plaster of Paris was mixed with water in a bucket, well stirred to break up lumps, and then poured gently (to avoid forming air bubbles) and gradually into the mould. Lengths of orthopaedic bandage (scrim dipped in plaster of Paris) were dipped in water and then pressed onto the back of the wet plaster. This strengthens the 'cast' considerably.

6 Once the plaster of Paris dried, approximately one hour, the wooden frame was dismantled, then the plaster and clay mould were carefully reversed onto a flat surface. Then the still pliable clay base was peeled off to reveal perfect impressions, in relief, of knobbly, crinkled half-nuts.

GLOSSARY OF TERMS & PRODUCTS

Acetate Clear, brittle plastic sheet. Can be drawn or printed on and used to check the alignment of motifs. Available from art and design materials suppliers.

Acrylic paint Synthetic, water-based paint available in very wide colour ranges in handy-sized tubes. It is fast drying and can be diluted with water. The paint provides a sealed surface and is an effective, permanent fabric paint. Available from art and design suppliers and craft shops.

Balsa wood Extremely lightweight wood of an American tropical tree. It is easy to cut and sand and its main use is in scale model making. Available from hobby and craft shops.

Beckmann's or RIT colour-run remover Manufacturers' names for a chemical compound containing sodium hydrosulphate. Used to strip the dye from fabric.

Calico Coarse, cheap cotton cloth. It comes either unbleached (a cream colour) or in white. Must be washed before use because it shrinks, but is good for printing as inks and paints are absorbed well without 'bleeding'. Available from upholstery suppliers and general fabric merchants.

Chipboard Reconstructed timber sheet made from wood chippings. It can be cut to any shape or size. It is an inexpensive material that can be nailed or drilled; having no grain, it will not split. Available from timber merchants.

Colourwash Proprietary colourwashes are produced, notably by Paint Magic. Colourwash is a water- or oil-based paint which is applied over a ground colour to give plenty of texture. Proprietary colourwash base coats and varnishes are also available.

Deka fabric paints Manufacturer's name for acrylic fabric paints that are water soluble when wet and water resistant when dry. They can be applied with a brush or used for printing. Most fabric paints have the same qualities; some need to be sealed with a hot iron, following manufacturer's instructions. Available from art and craft shops.

Dowel Cylindrical rods of wood that are sold in a range of diametres and lengths. Timber merchants stock most sizes, apart from the very finest, which are availble from model-making shops.

Fabric printing inks Thick acrylic colours for printing on fabric. 'Ink' in this case is the term used to describe colour applied by the print method, not transparent liquid ink.

Ferrous sulphate Basically, this is rust. The dust of corroded iron filings, used as a rust-brown fabric dye.

Flow Enhancer A proprietary liquid additive which gives 'slip' and longer working time to acrylic colours.

Frosting Medium A proprietary product devised by Paint Magic. It is applied to the surface of clear glass and gives the appearance of sand-blasting or etching. Available from Paint Magic stores or by mail order.

Greaseproof paper Paper that is impermeable to grease, also known as baking parchment. Makes good, cheap tracing paper. Available in food stores and supermarkets.

Impact adhesive Standard 'clear glue' sold under various brand names, UHU, for instance. It is a strong, multi-purpose glue that sticks most dry surfaces together and is both completely transparent and fast setting.

Japan Gold A size, or adhesive, traditionally used for attaching gold or other metal leaf to any surface.

Liquitex Glossies Manufactured by Binney & Smith Inc. in the U.S.A. Acrylic enamel paints that can be painted onto most surfaces. Their special quality is an excellent ceramic paint that can be baked in a domestic oven to make them permanent (although product disclaimers prevent the manufacturer from saying this). Available from art and craft shops.

Ocaldo water-based inks Brand name of inks in a range of colours that can be diluted with water.

Oiled manila stencil card Stencil material that is water resistant. The oil-soaked card cuts like cheese and is a delight to use. Transparent plastic stencil material has the advantage of making alignment and cornering much easier and is now popular. Stencil card has the advantage of being cheaper and easier to cut.

Print table A sturdy table customized for printing by covering it with a blanket and a top sheet of light canvas or calico. The two layers are pulled taught and tacked down to provide a sympathetic, springy surface for all types of printing.

Procion MX dyes Manufacurer's name for dyes, also known as fabric reactive dyes. These are chemical dyes that bond with the fibres. Fabrics are dipped into a bucket or tub of the diluted dye mixture. Available from art and craft shops.

PVA Polyvinyl acetate. Also known as white glue or wood-working glue. This marvellous stuff is a truly multi-purpose product. It can be used as an adhesive, a varnish, a binder and a sealant, and dilutes with water. Sold everywhere.

Rotring rubber Designer quality eraser that has a good texture for stamp cutting. Available from art and design shops, it can be substituted with any good quality eraser.

Shellac A methylated spirit-based varnish. It is fast-drying but not waterproof. Useful for sealing the surface of wood. Available from DIY stores, builders' merchants and iron-mongers (hardware stores).

Softening brush Used for softening out brushmarks. The finest are made of badger hair.

Spraymount An aerosol adhesive that does not give a permanent bond but allows for lifting and repositioning. Available from art and design materials suppliers.

Squeegee A strip of rubber mounted onto a wooden handle. Used for screen printing, it is grasped with both hands and dragged firmly across the screen to spread an even coating of ink. Available from art and printing materials suppliers.

Stanley knife Round handled, heavy-duty craft knife with replaceable blades. Stanley is a brand name. Available in all DIY stores, builders' merchants, craft shops, etc.

Stencil bridges Small tags that join the various elements of a stencil design. The simplest stencil is a cut-out shape, but bridges allow for shapes within shapes. They must be strong enough to hold the pieces together, but not so thick as to intrude upon the design.

Transfer metal leaf Squares of metal leaf mounted on sheets of waxed tissue, available in booklets and easier to handle than loose leaf.

Washing soda Large crystals mainly used as a household cleaning product. Soda is sodium carbonate and water. There is no exact U.S. equivalent product, apparently because of the relatively moderate melt-down temperature of the crystals.

Wooden stretching frame A cheap timber frame used in batik printing to hold the fabric clear of the work surface. This prevents the wax from dripping through then spreading back upwards.

Wundasize A water-based size (liquid glue) used for gilding. It has the necessary quality of staying 'open', not drying quickly.

FURTHER READING

Bawden, Edward, *A Book of Cuts* (Text by McLean, Ruari), Scolar Press, London, 1979

1800 Woodcuts by Thomas Bewick, Dover, New York, 1962

Binyon, Helen, *Eric Ravilious*, Lutterworth Press, Cambridge, 1983

Calloway, Stephen, *English Prints for the Collector,* Lutterworth Press, Cambridge, 1980

Dennis, Richard, *Ravilious and Wedgwood*, Dalrymple Press, Somerset, 1986

Elliott, Inger McCabe, *Batik, Fabled Cloth of Java*, Viking, New York, 1985

Robinson, Stuart, *A History of Printed Textiles*, Studio Vista, London, 1969

Hoskins, Lesley (ed.), *The Papered Wall*, Thames and Hudson, London, 1994

Lane, Richard, *Images from the Floating World*, Konecky and Konecky, New York, 1978

Russ, Stephen, *Fabric Printing by Hand*, Studio Vista, London, 1964

Samuel, Evelyn, *Introducing Batik*, Batsford, London, 1968

Schwab, Dean J., *Osaka Prints*, John Murray, London, 1989

Steinberg, S. H., *Five Hundred Years of Printing*, British Library and Oak Knoll Press, London, 1996

Storey, Joyce, *A Manual of Textile Printing*, Thames and Hudson, London, 1974 (new ed., 1992)

Walklin, Colin, *Relief Printmaking*, Crowood, Marlborough, 1991

Wechsler, Herman J., *Great Prints and Printmakers*, Thames and Hudson, London, 1967

PHOTOGRAPHIC ACKNOWLEDGEMENTS

All photographs by Graham Rae, except:

Caroline Bates/Impact Photos, p. 73; Thierry Bouzac/Impact Photos, pp. 6 (below), 22 (below), 71; Chelmsford Museum Service/Bridgeman Art Libarary, London, pp. 107, 110; Christie's Images/Bridgeman Art Library, London, p. 17; Tony Deane/Impact Photos, p. 74; Ben Edwards/Impact Photos, p. 173; Mary Evans Picture Library, London, p. 10; Fitzwilliam Museum, University of Cambridge/Bridgeman Art Library, London, pp. 9, 12; Jacqui Hurst, pp. 11, 108, 109; J. C. K. Archive, London/Bridgeman Art Library, London, p. 72; Caroline Jones, pp. 22 (above), 23; Alan Keohane/ Impact Photos, p. 20; Harvey Male/Impact Photos, p. 6 (above); Caroline Penn/Impact Photos, pp. 21, 89; Private Collections/ Bridgeman Art Library, London, pp. 13, 27; Dominic Sansoni/ Impact Photos, pp. 90, 158; Science Museum, London/ Bridgeman Art Library/ London, pp. 24; Stapleton Collection/ Bridgeman Art Library, London, pp. 7, 14; Victoria and Albert Museum, London/Bridgeman Art Library, London, pp. 28 (twice), 71, 124.